UNDERCOVER
ENVIRONMENTALISTS

UNDERCOVER
ENVIRONMENTALISTS

LYNDON STROTHER

ARCHWAY
PUBLISHING

Archway Publishing books may be ordered
through booksellers or by contacting:

Archway Publishing
1663 Liberty Drive
Bloomington, IN 47403
www.archwaypublishing.com
1 (888) 242-5904

ISBN: 978-1-4808-5495-6 (sc)
ISBN: 978-1-4808-5496-3 (hc)
ISBN: 978-1-4808-5497-0 (e)

Library of Congress Control Number: 2017916936

Print information available on the last page.

Archway Publishing rev. date: 11/1/2017

Contents

CHAPTER 1
Vigilante

Nobody pays much attention as he pulls up his truck in the field. Probably some inspector doing his job. He walks over to the big valve. It's a gate valve, buried in the ground. You can't see the pipe it controls. The wheel that operates the valve is a couple of feet in diameter. It's not chained. It doesn't budge at first—probably hasn't been used lately. Eventually he gets the big hand wheel to turn. It takes about twenty full rotations to close the valve. Halfway through closing the valve, a crew of workmen pass by in a pickup. Nobody even looks his way. They assume he belongs there. He is dressed for the part: hard hat, safety goggles, orange vest, work boots, and jeans. The other workers passing by don't even make eye contact. *This is good,* he thinks to himself. Like a man about his business, he heads back to his truck, gets in, and drives off.

About the time Bob is halfway home, just an hour's drive, all hell is breaking loose back at the plant, and they can't figure out why. The entire process facility shuts down. That was the twenty-four-inch waste line that runs a mile out in the ocean. Now the whole plant is backed up!

A month later, Bob heads back to the plant, but this time he's dressed like a lawyer. Always dress for the part! He enters the waiting room. You can tell it's a high-end, lucrative chemical corporation. In a bowl at the receptionist counter, they have synthetic silk matches, with the names of ships on each match—their ships.

Bob asks to see the manager. The receptionist asks his name. Yes, he called. Yes, he has an appointment.

The manager appears shortly and greets Bob. "Who did you say you were with?"

Bob responds, "Acme Chemical Waste Disposal Systems. We engineer reclaiming systems. What do you do with your waste by-products?"

The manager replies, "Oh, we pipe it out. It goes to a treatment facility."

"So one of your competitors buys it? If you ever decide to modify the system, feel free to have one of our engineers give you an estimate.". Bob hands the manager his card. "Guess you won't be needing our services right now. Thanks for taking the time to see me. Say, do you have a bathroom I could use?"

The manager says, "Yeah, down the hall and on the left." The manager makes no connection between Bob's inquiry and the previous month's upset, and he heads back to his office.

In the bathroom, Bob pulls fluorescent yellow packing peanuts out of several pockets, and he flushes them down the toilet. Meanwhile, unbeknownst to the big plant or its manager, a local TV camera crew is out in a small boat near where the pipe dumping out in the ocean ends. Tomorrow is going to be a bad day for the big plant and its manager!

It's evening. Bob's parks his truck at a different plant a whole state away. He's parked quite some distance from the facility and sets out for the plant on foot. There's a massive smokestack at one corner of the property. He heads straight for it, keeping it between himself the rest of the facility. Bob gets quite a workout. He thinks to himself, *And this is the easy part? I should have gotten help.* It took four hours to get there, but no one has noticed. Quite a view! The smokestack's red flashing warning lights are right next to him. It's amazing how many people driving around and even walking by fail to notice him. People don't look up, they look ahead. The red flashing light that looked so small from a mile away flashes silently. As he pulls up on the rope hand over hand, there is nothing on his mind but to get off the hot three-hundred-foot chimney. He stops pulling momentarily as a car's headlights flash across the base of the massive brick structure; it seems more like four hundred feet high. With the pulley on the giant homemade twenty-foot-diameter sheet metal "bottle top," he only has to lift half the weight, but there is six hundred feet of rope, and his arms are getting tired. Pulling up the giant "bottle cap" was hard, it's 12 foot across, but positioning it over the huge opening is the real challenge. Black smoke everywhere! Finally, he gets it tied off.

Now the easy part: the getaway. It may have taken four hours to get up, but any experienced climber can repel down in under a minute. He packs up the climbing gear and ropes. The trip back to the truck is a cake walk without that massive bottle cap. He sees flashlights around the base of the chimney as he's putting away the last item and climbing into the cab of his pickup. He's a mile away, and no one is even looking in his direction. Back to the house; his work is done.

Sometime later, the FBI catches up with Bob. Now Bob has a new job. It's not near as daring, let alone physically demanding. He sets up a big tripod. The camera he attaches to it has a built-in chronometer. He takes two pictures a couple of minutes apart. Now Bob works for the EPA! Those photos will be used as evidence in a federal court.

His real name isn't Bob, but he did pull off some spectacular feats, and he did go to work for the government.

CHAPTER 2
Undercover Work

In order to be effective as an undercover agent, you have to really get into the part. Actors do that for realism. They try to think of themselves as actual people who would do whatever the part requires. It's think, live, and be a tough guy—or think, live, and be a lawyer. The best way to learn about a business is to work in it. Want to know what really goes on behind closed doors in the media? Go to work for a radio station, TV station, or newspaper. Read everything you can get your hands on that pertains to the business. Besides that, you learn a bunch of interesting stuff, and you get a much more realistic perspective of what is going on in that particular business.

I worked at a radio station, a newspaper, and a huge commercial printer. I read several biographies on people like Walter Cronkite, the longtime TV anchorman, and Katherine Graham, a reporter, editor, Pulitzer Prize winner, and owner of the *Washington Post*. I am most definitely not an investigative reporter; I'm from the academic world. I was employed in the blue-collar world. When you are surrounded by ignorant rednecks who believe all sorts of stuff that isn't true, carry guns, and are likely to punch you out for saying something they don't like, you try to blend in, cut your hair, and wear a ball cap. You have to learn to ignore all the racists, sexists, and foul language. Wear the uniform, and pretend to be one of them.

I was an electrician, electrical troubleshooter, designer, and inspector. There are not too many businesses in which I haven't worked. If you want to know how something works, ask a control electrician. He's hooked up printing presses, injecting molding, automated machining, bottling, canning, and all manners of process and manufacturing machines. After you install and wire up a new machine or system, you often have a more thorough understanding of it than the future operators of that machine or system. Practically everything in industry has a dependence on electricity. After you build and install a new machine or system, you have to stick around and see that it works. This is called functional checkout (FCO), or acceptance testing. It is often performed by an independent third party. After the construction is substantially complete, you double-check everything and operate the machine or system to all its extremes to make sure everything works like it was designed. One then hands off the completed system or process to its new owner. For lights, you simply turn them on and leave them on. For more complex process systems, you get it working and then try to trip up the system. One of the primary reasons for doing this is that the owner is likely to put people who are not so skilled in charge of operating the machine or system. Believe me—if people can screw up, they will. Making the process or system idiot-proof becomes a priority. The bigger and more complex the process or machine is, the more it costs and the more serious mistakes can be. Many of the more serious process systems have the equivalent of armies of computers, as well as multiple operators to monitor and control the process. Shutting down some systems in the event of an upset will require a specific sequence to shut it down properly. Failure to do so could result in fire, explosions, hazard waste spills, death, and destruction. Insurance companies don't like that, and so they send around inspectors like me to attempt to protect their investments.

My association with the petrochemical industry started with the suppliers. After working for several suppliers and subcontractors, I did some additions to refineries. This was new construction. In my business, which was the power to run the big pumps, elaborate fire and gas detection systems, fire suppression systems, lighting, and the controls, one needs to have a fairly thorough understanding of what is going on and is supposed to happen. Once you become well seasoned in a particular science, art, or industry, it's pretty easy to get around without raising suspicion. If you know what you are doing and are pretty "about your business," people don't pay much attention to you. I knew what I was doing; I belonged there.

I heard this one story about some town that was looking into using the digester gasses off a wastewater treatment plant to run a turbine and produce electricity. This was in the seventies. As the story went, the engineering firm that did the feasibility study had concluded that it was not practical or economical. That engineering firm was supposedly owned by one of the big oil companies. The heart of the rumor was that the oil company did it just to discourage efficiency. The Swiss had been using their methane from their wastewater treatment plants to produce electricity since the fifties. Efficient reuse of waste gas would have been a recurring theme in trade journals that deal with that sort of thing. Over time, I learned to pick out the conspiracy theorists with their wild stories that were not based on facts or actual occurrences. Of course, being there trumps gossip any day. I'm not a big fan of gossip; I'm more a fan of Ben Franklin's way of thinking. He had his own version of the Ten Commandments, and one of them was "Speak not but what may benefit others or yourself; avoid trifling conversation." This was directed specifically against gossip.

CHAPTER 3

Becoming a True Tree Hugger

I was born near the Everglades. Florida has a lot of swamps, and they are the primordial soup of creation. There are also a lot of things that bite there—mosquitoes, ants, spiders, scorpions, snakes, turtles, and alligators. I visited the Okefenokee, another big park at the Florida-Georgia border. It ranks as one of the larger swamps in the world. We counted over a hundred alligators in the first hour we were there. Some were big, about fifteen feet long, with wicked bad breath and hide that the prop from the outboard motor on our boat didn't even cut. Florida has 161 state parks and 11 national parks.

Florida even has an underwater park, the first in the nation: John Pennenkamp Coral Reef State Park, in Key Largo. I went on a dive there, wandered away from my dive partner, and encountered a huge emerald-green moray eel. I'd seen lots of smaller morays in the Bahamas and off the coast of Mexico, but I'd only heard about the rare emerald green ones. Most of what I'd seen were army camo, black and olive. When you are scuba diving, you have to wear an inflatable vest called a buoyancy compensator, or BC for short, to offset the weight of the tanks and your other gear. You wear additional weights and inflate and deflate the vest to adjust your weight according to the depth you are at. This allows you to remain stationary at various depths. If you don't go up and down too much, after adjusting the BC, you can control your depth by breathing control. I was getting tired of constantly adjusting the BC and spotted some huge steel sections; they were the hull of an ore ship. It had gotten hung up in the reef, and they had dynamited it into smaller pieces. The park is all protected coral, and some of it is poisonous. Touching it is not only a violation of park rules but can be quite painful and hazardous to one's health. I had these huge, three-foot-long fins on that made it easy to get around, and I headed over to the wreck. I settled down on the edge of the three-quarter-inch-thick steel plate.

From directly under me comes this massive green eel. It was beautiful but rather intimidating. Like sharks, morays always swim with their mouths open, to allow water to pass over their gills. And they have teeth—lots of teeth. This thing came to within a foot or two of my face, so I'm looking right down its throat. Obviously other divers had been feeding it, and it was looking for treats, but I didn't have any. Its head was roughly the size of mine, and it had to be eight feet or longer. It was probably twenty-four to thirty inches from top fin to bottom fin. Finally, it determined that I didn't have any treats and wandered off. Adrenaline was dripping out my fingers, and my heart was up somewhere around my throat.

I worked in Alaska for twenty-one years. Alaska has 120 state parks and 24 national parks. One in particular, Wrangell/St. Alias, is one of the largest parks in the world. Collectively, Alaska's parks cover an area that is larger than most states. Just Wrangell St. Elias, Denali, Gates of the Arctic, NOATAK, and ANWR, at 193,996 square kilometers together, would rank as the fifteenth largest state, roughly as big as the nine smallest US states combined. ANWR alone is as big as the five smallest states combined. One county in Alaska, called the North Slope Borough, is as large as the ten smallest states combined. If it was a state, it would be the twelfth-largest state! ANWR, the Arctic National Wildlife Refuge, falls in its borders. The borough also includes part of the gates of the Arctic National Park and Preserve and the NOATAK National Preserve. A majority of my time in Alaska was spent somewhere on the North Slope.

I've visited many of the US and Canadian national parks and monuments. The list would be at least a page, and it would be boring reading.

I got a cat when I was in first grade, and then I started collecting bugs. Next it was snakes. I had ten to fifteen snakes at a time. They were in little cages, like Radar from MASH. All were nonpoisonous. I had this little blue racer that bit me every time I tried to pick him up. I decided right then and there not to mess with poisonous species, but I still got alarmingly close to them.

Then I started feeding a wild alligator. We called him Ally Alligator, and he would come when we called him. He lived in a small pond on the campus of the University of Florida. He would eat anything—bread, cheese, steak, dogs ... But he would only come for me and my sister when we called him. I never figured out how he could hear us underwater. He was about five feet long. Dogs would see him and jump right in the water—and that the last one would see of them!

Later, when I moved north to Massachusetts, I had more pets. I had dogs, skunks, squirrels, chipmunks, rabbits, red squirrels, and flying squirrels. Last but not least, I had a giant desert tortoise. It was at a missile test site near Death Valley National Monument. We only kept him a year and then let him go back in the desert. There were so many sidewinders there that one didn't dare walk at night. In the morning, there would be tracks everywhere. Sidewinders have a most interesting method of locomotion. They are one of the only species of snake in North America that can navigate the sandy desert. They skate along at forty-five degrees to the direction of their body. Other snakes can't handle sand; they get stuck like a car with narrow tires. What most people don't know is that they can strike one and a half times their length! From coiled, most venomous snakes can only strike about two-thirds of their length, but a sidewinder can spring much further when not coiled. They are territorial, so we gave them a wide berth. Snakes can be aggressive too. I've been chased by a puff adder and by a very small rattlesnake.

We had a tree farm in Georgia, and I worked on it during the summers. One had to wear protective leggings and carry a snake bite kit there. When a local hunter killed a twelve-foot rattlesnake on our property, I was skeptical. I had handled and dealt with reptiles, and I had some books, so that I knew what to feed them and how to care for them. It was a big diamondback, and they may be interbred with timber rattlers. According to my snake guide, those two species maxed out at about eight feet. In a later, perhaps tenth edition, it said, "Slightly larger in South Georgia." I was in third grade at the time, and I remember looking at the metal and cloth snake leggings and thinking, *A hell of a lot of good these will do me! That thing could reach up and bite me on my jugular vein!* It weighed in at over sixty pounds.

Back at home, which was always some big university, one of my associates had a family where both the husband and the wife were PhD marine biologists. They used to dive with Jacques Cousteau and had all sorts of pictures from hanging out with him and his sons on the *Calypso*. The professor also had an algae named after him. Another buddy's folks were both PhD botanists. The father in that family was voted the most popular teacher many years in a row and had coauthored a botany text with some other professors that was being used to teach Botany 101 at hundreds of universities across the nation. Their son and I spent a lot of time wandering through the labs and in the greenhouses of the botany department. We also spent time in the botany library doing research.

Some of my cohorts studied at Woods Hole. I visited there twice. I got interested in solar power and wind power in the late sixties. MIT wasn't too far away, and I got a commercial user's card through a friend of my dad's for a birthday present. I started using the library when I was fourteen and continued using it until I was twenty-three. In all, I probably spent thirty to forty eight-hour days, and that many more partial days in the MIT library. It was probably more time than some of the registered students spent there. There were four dominant solar journals, one American, one Russian, one Israeli, and one Arabic or Egyptian. Solar research journals didn't exist much before the fifties. I flipped through every copy. I didn't read every article, but I read a lot of articles. MIT's library had books that had been translated—a real plus if one didn't speak Russian or Arabic. Solar wasn't the only thing I studied. I flipped through the entire IEEE journal from its inception in the 1800s, as well as all of the *Bell System Technical Journal*. At the library, located at 77 Mass Avenue, was this interesting, two-part study on the building of the Trans-Siberian Power line. It's a three-thousand-mile-long power line that at the time was the longest and highest voltage power line in operation. The first book detailed the construction; the second volume was a ten-year study on the operation and maintenance. It worked at three-quarters of a million volts and had massive towers and insulator chains. Previously, the highest voltage power line in the world was one out of Grand Coulee, operating at 525,000 volts and later upgraded to 600,000 Volts. The study was one of only two copies in the

United States and had been translated from Russian to English at quite some cost. They failed to translate the captions for various photos, but it was usually pretty easy to infer what was being indicated. There were great pictures of the Urals and some massive hydroelectric dams, as well as details of crushed rail and damaged bridges from the weight of massive transformers and turbines being installed on that project. For the Russians, it was a project in league with our building of the Grand Coulee Dam or the Tennessee Valley Authority.

In high school, I wrote my first research paper on battery technology. The majority of the report was more a historical overview of battery history and developments. But as an avid reader with access to technical journals not available at the local newsstand, I included stuff on the most recent developments of the time. They had just invented the sulfur/sodium cell, and the lithium chloride looked promising. These new batteries didn't actually show up on the commercial market for another thirty years. I had incorrectly assumed that battery technology would develop along the lines of More's Law—the one about computing power and memory capacity doubling every nine months. As I observed back then, batteries were the Achilles heel of electric cars, which we should have developed much earlier, and much more ardently, years ago.

One year I was in Phoenix, Arizona, and checked out the solar library collection at ASU. There was interesting stuff there, some of which one might not find in the Library of Congress. The solar collection may be unmatched anywhere else in the world.

I have worked for almost every state and federal agency except the CIA, NSA, and FBI. The list includes FHMA, ASCS, National Park Service, National Wildlife Service, BLM, National Forest Service, Soil Conservation Commission, Army, Navy, Air Force, Marines, National Guard, Coast Guard, Strategic Air Command,

Federal Reserve Bank, Animal Damage Control, Bonneville Power Administration, and JPO. I even did a bit of work at some classified locations with the US Border Patrol and places like the fabled Area 51.

I have two associates who work on oceanographic research ships, and at least a dozen professional associates who are environmental inspectors. Having had such a wide variety of pets, I was also a regular at the local veterinary hospital. I built a large veterinary hospital that had three full-time vets and a staff of twenty-six more people. They had an electron microscope, a live ultrasound scanner, two x-ray machines, and an operating theatre with three stations. It had real operating lights overhead that were from a people's hospital, and I installed them. It definitely wasn't your run-of-the-mill veterinary hospital. Most vets didn't have most of this stuff. They were probably the only private veterinary hospital in the United States to own an electron microscope. The vet who dealt with all the big animals—livestock like horses, cows, and sheep—had two mobile units that could go out in the field and do operations on-site. He made house calls! They were without question the most advanced veterinary operation I had ever witnessed. They were the first to computerize in the early eighties, and they kept a university student busy all day, every day, entering data in their own mainframe data bank. The vet was a Cornell grad. Cornell was one of the top, if not *the* top, veterinary school. He would scan through veterinary journals and highlight the articles, and then the students would enter the material in his database. If someone brought in an animal with a rare or obscure disease, he had a much better chance of correctly diagnosing it and knowing what the appropriate treatment was. He should have been awarded a Nobel Prize for his efforts in this direction.

I've built and worked on greenhouses. I've also toured and

inspected some fantastic greenhouses with huge botanical collections. They smell neat and probably have higher oxygen levels than outside. And of course, they are full of all these neat collections of plants and flowers. They are a great place to get away from the rat race of the city or to take a date for a walk.

In fourth grade, we built some greenhouses out of the nose section of fighter jets. After installing lights and an astronomical timer, we were able to get roses to bloom around Christmas. It was in Gainesville, Florida, at the P. K. Young Experimental School, where stuff grows pretty well even without a greenhouse.

Last but not least in my experience in environmental studies, I have worked on farms. I've picked beans and berries, milked cows, baled hay, harvested rye, and shoveled manure. One of the most innovative things I've come across while working at a big, experimental farm was the use of predatory insects instead of pesticides. They raised the bugs that ate other bugs. Pretty cool!

I've hiked most of the Appalachian Trail, and I've climbed lots of mountains. I'm often accompanied by a geologist or someone with a lot of knowledge about the wilderness. Even though my main vocation has been electromechanical engineering, I have a bit of knowledge in the environmental arena. A recent study claims that to attain the equivalent of a master's degree in a subject, one has to put in so many thousands of hours. I've put in the hours in several fields. As an electrical troubleshooter, I had to look at and understand the workings of complex manufacturing and production machinery. If it has electricity associated with it, I've probably built, installed, tested, inspected, or troubleshot it. I may not have a degree in environmental science, but I have the hours in experience, and I definitely know a bit more about it than most of the population of the planet. And I'm still learning. Between my work experience, what I've read, and what I learned from my peers in the life sciences and environmental arena, I probably am somewhere between a bachelor's and master's in environmental science.

Automated material handling, processing, and packaging of food products involve a lot of what I do. I've gone from grain elevators and traveling showers in soybean facilities, fruit processing, dairy, baking, meat, and produce packaging and handling, to huge dough mixers and giant ovens. It's quite a long list that includes practically every type of manufacturing.

> **It is better to hang out with people better than you. Pick out associates whose behavior is better than yours and you'll drift in that direction.**
> **—Warren Buffett**

I can personally attest to the truth in Mr. Buffett's words of wisdom. In the college and university scene in which I was born and grew up, the kid whose parents were English professors knew more English than many college grads did—and this was by the time they were ten years old. Likewise, the botany professor's kid knew more about the life sciences by the time he was twelve than most people learned in a lifetime. I grew up with mathematicians. Math is tied to almost every science and a lot of other subjects as well. All the heavy sciences like mechanical, electrical, civil, and aeronautical engineering need math. Physics and chemistry do too. Many of the life sciences lean heavily on statistics. Math is like a central hub for many fields. Many of the best and brightest scientists get a master's degree in math, and then a doctorate in their specific areas of interest, such as physics, astronomy, and now computer science. My interest was mostly science. By being around so many people in the sciences, I got a pretty good formal and informal education in environmental science. Being an avid reader has advanced my knowledge in many fields as well.

ALWAYS ASK QUESTIONS!

In construction, you have lots of folks who are not inclined to ever ask questions. They think asking a question is admitting that they don't know something and are likely to get ostracized or reprimanded. What a big mistake! Both groups—the ones who don't ask, and the ones who make fun of or reprimand those who ask questions—are idiots. How are you going to learn?

For a kid interested in the sciences, growing up at colleges and universities that had great specialty libraries and laboratories was like growing up at Disneyland. I had a very specialized MO. I initially developed my routine at the age of nine or ten years old and refined it from there. At the university, there would be students who were working on their master's or doctorate degree, and they were a bit more serious about their studies than the average student. On weekends and holidays, when other students were on vacation, these dedicated students would be there working. Some couldn't afford to fly home to India or California. I would wander into their labs. Meek—that was the key. I would wander in, ask if I could look around, promise not to touch anything, and look at all the neat glassware and lab equipment. "What does that do?"

"Well, that's a 50,000 G centrifuge. See—we take this rat, nuke it with radiation, toss it in the blender, and then put the liquefied material in these tiny buckets that go in the centrifuge. Then we pump all the air out. The fifty thousand Gs separates the various materials into these layers. In a test tube, it looks kind of like one of those layered drinks. Then we take a Pipet and draw out the DNA from this layer."

While other kids my age were fishing or playing baseball, I was learning about DNA at a time when the only people who knew about it were generating the first articles in *Scientific American* and technical journals. My experience in this was limited to the University of Miami, Miami Florida; Miami University, Oxford, Ohio; Stanford, in California; the University of Florida, Gainesville; the University of Nevada, Reno; the University of Georgia, Athens; the University of Massachusetts, Amherst; Amherst College; Greenfield Community College, Greenfield, Massachusetts; the University of Washington, Seattle; Green River Community College, Auburn, Washington; and Montana State, Bozeman. I visited and studied at roughly fifty more colleges and universities in the United States and Canada.

NOT CHEMISTRY!

I touched base with most of the life sciences, from one-celled critters and plants to the more complex animal kingdom. However, I never liked chemistry, and this field overlaps a good deal with the life sciences. Initially, my dislike for chemistry came from a Christmas present I got when I was eleven years old. It was a Gilbert chemistry set. They came in various models, and I got a "two-door" model, not the top-of-the-line model. I started doing the first exercises in the little handbook that came with it. The second or third experiment required me to filter a solution through filter paper. At this time, Dr. Strother (never Dad or Pa) sauntered over and related a story about how some associate of his, a chemist, took two years to filter some solution on which he was working. That was it—I lost interest in chemistry right then and there.

I liked electricity. There was instant gratification. It was invisible and powerful. Hit the switch, and on comes the light. I had already built a small electric motor when I was eight. Further experiences playing in and around the chemistry, biology, and botany laboratories reinforced my dislike of chemistry. They smelled funny and often had signs noting biological hazards, chemical hazards, and radiation hazards everywhere. Acids and poisons were nasty stuff. I later became familiar with some research places like Plum Island, a biological warfare research facility. I found these biological and chemical warfare research places to be scarier than nuclear stuff. Nuclear and even chemical places didn't have the ability to spread at exponential rates like diseases did. If you are a Star Trek fan, you might have picked up on the Klingon symbol used at the end of radio transmissions: it was the biohazard symbol! Cute, but not for me. I suppose somewhere in the definition of life, part of the definition should include "Grows at an exponential rate."

In later years, I had a series of bad experiences with chlorine and nitric acid. It was the late fifties, and I was at a hotel across the street from Disney Land, in California. I was about six. We had just driven from Miami after school let out, which was also around my birthday. It was a long haul—three thousand miles. They were in the process of building the interstate highway system. We didn't have an air-conditioned car. But because we were from the South, we were fairly accustomed to hot weather. I jumped in to the pool at the hotel. At the far end of the pool, a teenage kid had just tipped a fifty-gallon drum over, and a thin film was forming on the water. The manager came running out and screamed at the young man. They tipped the drum back up. Probably a third of the drum had run into the pool. He informed the young man, "That was pure chlorine. You were only supposed to put in a quart!" When I exited the pool, my skin began to burn, and I was as bright red as a lobster. I was hospitalized with a severe chemical burn from head to toe. Definitely not a happy camper!

I got a serious burn from nitric acid in my mid-twenties. I was wiring up this acid etching machine in Phoenix, Arizona. The customer didn't bother to caution me and my helper about the twenty liters of twelve-molar nitric in the machine. I brushed up against the intake fill tube. Less than a minute later, my foot was itching. I look down to see an eighteen-inch-long triangle of my jeans, from my sneaker to my knee, smoking. The whole side of my sneaker is gone, and smoke was coming off my foot! Not fun!

In the refining business, they use an acid in various forms that is extremely deadly. Hydrofluoric acid, not to be confused with hydrochloric acid, is like the Alien blood from the movies. It eats through almost anything: steel, concrete … and human flesh. In high enough strength, it acts quite quickly. Most acids don't eat through glass, so that is what they are stored in. Hydrofluoric gets stored in wax-lined plastic bottles. Fumes produced by it are highly toxic and account for many refinery fatalities.

ABOUT TREES

Trees are neat. They furnish us with lumber, give squirrels and birds a place to live, and create oxygen. The Cudlees and the Druids worshipped trees. They also are what the first ships were made of, which opened up the exploration of our planet. There are some impressive cypress in the Okefanokee Swamp, which straddles the Florida-Georgia border. They are close to three thousand years old and live submerged in a few feet of water. If the water were to go away, the trees would die. This tells us that the environment there has stayed fairly stable for many thousands of years. Redwoods are impressive as well. It's a long climb up to the nest if you are a squirrel living in one of these. The whole northwest has beautiful, great big trees. Some of the northwest's trees are believed to hold the record for height, and 379 feet is certainly much taller than any trees where I grew up in Florida, Georgia, Ohio, or Massachusetts. Near where I currently live, nestled in between the Olympic Forest and Mt. Rainier National Park, there is a tree stump from a tree that was roughly thirty feet in diameter. Some guy carved out the inside; put in a couple of windows and a door; added a square, trussed roof; and lived there while he built his real house. Now it's a gardening shed that's larger than many folks' living rooms.

Those who work in the timber industry are often very anti-environmentalist. Think about this: If you grew up in the Amazon rain forest, or in Washington, Oregon, Northern California, British Columbia, or southern Alaska, it looks like the whole world is trees. There is a tendency to assume the whole world is like where you grew up. But the reality is that 71 percent of the world is covered by water, 10 percent is covered by ice, and 14 percent is true desert, with another 15 percent being desert like. How can that be? That adds up to more than 100 percent! That's because some of the area covered by ice falls under the desert category. Loggers assume that trees are an indefinite resource and can't understand why they are being limited regarding how much they cut. What most people are completely unaware of is that in another part of the world, thousands of years ago, there was a thriving timber industry that vanished. That area is now the desert of Egypt. We almost did the same thing to what briefly became the Dust Bowl in the central United States.

It takes hundreds of thousands to millions of years for soil thick enough to support trees to form. You start with some somewhat sterile rock. Molds and moss grow on it for years and die, and then more grows on top of that. Then come grasses and ferns—stuff that a big wind storm won't blow away. After thousands of generations of smaller plants living and dying, you get bushes and finally trees.

There are no trees north of the Arctic Circle. There's not even much in the way of bushes, just some incredibly tough forms of grass that make up tundra. When one drives north along the Haul Road, Alyeska's highway from Fairbanks to Prudhoe Bay, as one approaches the Arctic Circle, the trees vanish. They can't grow in permafrost. The trees near the Arctic Circle are a species of pine that don't get very big. There's this big sign on the last tree that states, "Northern-most spruce tree on the Trans-Alaska Pipeline. Please do not cut." There are about six stumps just north of it where someone stole the tree, sign and all! I tried climbing this tree, and one of my coworkers got a picture. I was "the original tree hugger." It was a bit like being a sheep in wolf's clothing because all of my coworkers were oil workers who considered environmentalists to be Public Enemy Number One. As an electrical inspector, I was pretty well disguised.

CHAPTER 4

Contractor for Paradise

I was an electrical contractor in Massachusetts for eight years. At the same time, I was the electrical inspector for two towns, Leverett and Sunderland, Mass(short for Massachusetts; people from the area shorten it). In 1990, I sold off my business, turned in my badge as electrical inspector, and moved to the Seattle/Tacoma area of Washington. I ended up working for a subcontractor to Boeing, designing and building material handling systems—mostly bridge cranes used in the big aircraft assembly plants. Every weekend for the first year I lived there, roughly forty-three consecutive weekends, I climbed Mt. Rainier, a lofty fourteen-thousand-foot, glacier-covered mountain that is one of the first national parks. It was set aside as a national park at the same time Yellowstone was. Gifford Pinchot, John Muir, and Teddy Roosevelt, on horseback, toured what were to become the first national parks before they became parks.

At the base of Mt. Rainier is a small forest ranger town, with a museum, big storage buildings for equipment, and apartments and houses for the park employees. The town is called Longmire. There are a lot of fabulous trees there—really big trees. One species in particular, nobel pine, or nobel fir, is tall and straight, which was very desirable for ships masts. It only grows from the

Oregon-Washington border to the Canadian border at a very specific altitude. The park also has very large cedars, ones with bases up to twenty feet across. At Longmire, there is a gate that is closed in the evening and doesn't open until about eight in the morning. The road up to Paradise, at roughly six thousand feet elevation, is prone to avalanches and almost always has rocks and debris every morning, summer and winter. Paradise is the second highest place on Mt. Rainier you can drive to, and it has a visitor center and an old lodge. They send a couple of big Pass Plows up it to check it out and clean off the rock and debris in the summer, as well as snow in the winter. Snow banks there are often twenty feet high. I was waiting in an area where they parked the snow plows in some big shop buildings for the gate to be opened. I went there every weekend for about a year to hike up and ski down. I was in my Utility body three-quarter-ton truck. I alternated between driving that and a 1960 VW Bus, the trademark hippy vehicle.

I was reading the Sunday comics, and one of the big snow plows started up its diesel. A few minutes later, this huge, bearded guy whom one could easily have mistaken for Paul Bunyan pulls out, gets out of his truck, closes the shops doors, gets back in the plow truck, and pulls up next to me. He cranks his window down. "Contractor for Paradise?" Well I was a contractor, and I was going to Paradise, so I said yes. My truck had Washington Crane signs on the sides so that I could get into various Boeing plants. Personal vehicles were not allowed in the plants, but commercial vehicles were. With the signs on my truck and its utility body, it passed nicely as a commercial vehicle. It saved having to drag tools, ladders, and materials from some parking lot a mile away. But I'm pretty sure what the snow plow driver was actually asking was whether I was one of the contractors working on the renovation of some old lodge buildings up at the six-thousand-feet level, at Paradise. They opened the gate, he went through, I followed, another big snow plow fell in line behind me, and they closed and relocked the gate. I got a custom escort up to Paradise!

At the Stevens Canyon turnoff, the plow behind me turned off. When we got to Paradise, the driver who was in the lead waved and headed back down. They apparently never noticed the full-frame pack and two sets of skis in the back of my truck. I used thin Cross-X skis with goat hair skins to go up, which usually took about four to five hours. Tied on the pack were massive 220-centimeter downhill skis. In the pack were the downhill boots, each the size and weight of a concrete block. I could usually make the three-thousand-foot descent from Camp Muir to Paradise in less than twelve minutes. Four hours up, twelve minutes down. That day I was already a mile up the mountain before the twenty cars that had been waiting at the Longmire gate got up to the parking lot at Paradise. That made my day!

CHAPTER 5

Conspiracy

con·spir·a·cy, n., 1. a secret plan by two or more people to do something bad or unlawful.

That's according to Mr. Webster. The government and the law also use a similar definition. But neither of these parties say anything about doing something unethical. The government and the oil companies got clean away with it. "Got away with what?" you say. You get to be the judge on this one.

Between 1976 and 1980, I was a journeyman commercial electrician in Houston, Texas. I built a lot of grocery stores, restaurants, and drug stores. And of course, the Rice University Library was there too. One day I was with three other electricians standing in line in the post office, and my buddy was flipping though the Most Wanted list. He commented, "Hey, check it out. Of the ten most wanted by the FBI, seven either posed as or were electricians!"

I didn't have to pretend to be an electrician—I was born a master electrician! I built an electric motor when I was six, a radio when I was ten and a twenty-six-band transceiver when I was twelve. At fourteen, I wired my first house and got in trouble with the FCC for attempting to operate a fifty-kilowatt ex-military radar set. By the time I was in Houston, I was a foreman.

In 1977, things started to heat up on the construction of the

Trans-Alaska Pipeline. The oil industry of the world used to re-
volve around Houston, Texas. No matter where the oil field was—
Russia, Saudi Arabia, North Sea—the tooling and machinery, the
drill rigs, and the personnel all came from Houston. The biggest
oil tooling companies were in Houston: Brown Oil Tools, Dresser
Atlas, Hughes Tool, Cameron Iron Works. So were the big oil
companies. In most cities, the biggest buildings are insurance company buildings, like Prudential, John Hancock, Sears, and Allstate.
In Houston it's Exxon, Mobile, Chevron, Gulf, Shell, and Texaco.

Lots of folks from Texas were going up to Alaska, and the
money was attractive. I signed up with a job-placement service
that got people jobs on the Alaska Pipeline, gave them my fifty
dollars, filled out an application, and never heard from them again!
One day I went by their offices, and some guys were loading the
furniture out the door. They had packed up and split town! They
made off with some other kids' money. His uncle was a judge, and
he went after them and got it back. I wasn't as fortunate. My fifty
bucks was gone. I never did make it to Alaska during the construction of the pipeline.

There are two things I have in common with "Deep Throat,"
Woodward and Bernstein's inside-government source for Watergate.
One is that we share the same name, and the second is my dislike
of inaccuracy in reporting by some of the media. For years the
media, and to some extent the movie industry, have villainized
certain groups in order to sell their product. I can think of at least
a dozen movies that use the name of a scientist for a character and
portray them to be villains, when in reality those scientists were
more likely to be pacifists and people who valued honesty and integrity. It's appalling how many people firmly believe that in order
to be rich and successful, you must be evil. But in reality, many
rich folks are not dishonest, scheming criminals; they are actually

very hard-working, industrious, honest individuals. That doesn't sell tickets to the movie or newspapers on the stand, and so some of the media and much of the entertainment industry bend the right to freedom of expression into more the freedom to lie and deceive.

In Colin Powell's book *My American Journey*, he relates how a professional associate of his in the government warned him, "Never do battle with people who buy ink by the barrel!" This is a much older quote attributed to someone around Ben Franklin's time. Franklin did own a printing press. I was a web press technician for a while. Mostly what I did was troubleshoot complex electrical control systems associated with four multimillion-dollar printing presses. These were 120-foot-long, two-story-high, color-printing presses that required a gang of a dozen skilled technicians to operate. They generated picture-perfect, colored work like *Time* magazine or *National Geographic* at rates of up to thirty-two thousand impressions per hour. They were noisy, requiring double hearing protection, and they were complicated. Given the opportunity, I would have liked to have given Colin Powel a tour of one of these while it was operating. They have very complex, sophisticated, electrical controls. We did buy ink by the barrel—actually four barrels at a time: black, red, blue, and yellow. I installed an ultrasonic ink leveling system on one $12 million printing press. Then I could ask Colin Powell at the end of the tour, "So what's it like having those guys that buy ink by the barrel working for you?" His book was great, and I highly recommend it. It gives a more accurate view of the workings of government than is portrayed elsewhere, as well as a lot of good-sense advice that one can use in everyday life as well as at work. After having worked under presidents from both parties, his observations tend to be more accurate than some other folks.

In the 1920s, a couple of geologists spent a year dragging a canoe around what would later become the North Slope of Alaska. Various places there had signs of oil. Some lakes and ponds had trace amounts of oil on the water from natural leakage. In a few places, there were actual oil lakes. The native Alaskans would use the oil to coat boat hulls as a sealant. Then in the 1940s, the navy drilled some test holes and even ran some small, somewhat secret oil operations there. Finally in the 1960s, the federal government gave part of this land to the State of Alaska. Alaska immediately leased out sections of the land to oil companies, making Alaska one of the richest states overnight. Several oil companies started drilling, with limited success. Oil often occurs in thin layers that may only be twenty or fifty feet thick. If they were not paying attention, they could drill right through it and miss it. This happened a lot. Finally, Arco punched in a good, productive well. The oil is at depth of ten thousand feet, and one has to drill through three thousand feet of permafrost first to get there. The area the geologists mapped out in the 1920s became Navy Petroleum Reserve #4, and it's the size of Ohio, at thirty-three thousand square miles.

Once they found the oil, the next hurdle was how to get it off the North Slope. There was no road. The nearest city, Fairbanks, was five hundred miles south. The cheapest way to haul anything was by ship. The second most economical way was pipeline, third was rail, and the fourth was truck. The most expensive way was by air. In 1968, Humble Oil took what was one of the largest merchant ships of the time, the SS *Manhattan;* cut off the bow; stretched it a bit; reinforced it a bunch; and ended up with a thousand-foot-long, ice-cutting tanker. It was very much one of a kind. In 1969 the *Manhattan*, along with an escort of other smaller ice cutters, made it through the fabled Northwest Passage. Until that time, the Northwest Passage was only a legend. Many expeditions had failed, and many sailors and explorers died trying to find a way across the top of the globe; there was too much ice, and it was frozen practically year round. Though the *Manhattan* made it to become the first ship to successfully navigate a route through, there was massive damage to the ship. The entire event was overshadowed by the moon landing in July 1969, so most folks never knew it took place.

At this point, the oil companies started looking at other options. The railroad people wanted to build a rail line, and the teamsters wanted a six-lane freeway. However, the next most economical way was by pipeline. It is good that they didn't decide to go with the rail or truck options. Accidents would have spilled two hundred to five hundred times as much crude as the pipeline ultimately did. This is something many people don't bother to think about when they protest. What are the alternatives? Will they be more hazardous?

The oil companies BP, Arco, Phillips, Mobile, and some others joined forces and created the Alyeska Pipeline Service Company. Running a pipeline is overhead, not profit; it's simply a cost of doing business. As an oil company, one usually creates a spin-off, separate company for transportation, as well as for refining. Transporting oil and refining oil don't make money. *Selling* oil and its byproducts makes money! Shell, Gulf, Mobile, and the other oil companies separate off their pipeline companies for bookkeeping and tax purposes. The creation and building of the Alaska Pipeline was a bit bigger project than had previously been taken on by any company. In fact, it was the largest privately funded project in history up until that time. It was so big that it was the largest construction project since the Panama Canal. The oil companies, the largest companies in the world, had to borrow money to build it. The loan to build the TAPS (Trans-Alaska Pipeline Service) company was federally backed by Congress. It was a massive project with twelve pump stations, a huge marine terminal, and eight hundred miles of pipe. There are also eight hundred river and road crossings, so there are eight hundred bridges to inspect yearly. There are 125 massive valves to isolate sections of the pipeline in case there was a leak: before and after bridges and river crossings, and near seismic faults. About sixty-eight of them are remote, and these cost around $50 million apiece.

The engineering was basically copied from some existing pipelines that operated in the Mideast, but it required serious modifications because no one had ever run a pipeline across permafrost. After battling their way through permits with state and federal agencies, a deal was made with the Japanese for the pipe. On a handshake-type deal, the Japanese cut the oil companies a great deal on the pipe, contingent upon them later getting to purchase oil after it was completed.

As construction was ramping up, environmental groups got a court injunction to halt the building of the Trans-Alaska pipeline. They managed to shut it down for two years. This was where things started getting interesting. The poorly funded and poorly administered environmental groups never stood a chance. This can happen when you are going up against governments and companies that have vastly superior resources. They don't have to be that organized, and unlike in the movies, where they show oil company lawyers having Supreme Court judges executed by assassins, they don't have to do anything quite that clandestine or diabolical.

Much like Watergate, everyone was in on it, and it probably remains to this day one of the more perfectly arranged conspiracies. The "it" was an oil embargo—one that was staged!

I was an electrical and instrumentation inspector on the Alyeska Pipeline for seven years. I drove the length of the pipeline somewhere around five hundred times, half of the time on 'ice roads'. I worked at all twelve pump stations and had offices at the start, in Prudhoe Bay, and in the middle, in Fairbanks. Where the pipe leaves Pump One, there is a big "0 mile" marker sign. The pipe is buried, and where it emerges from the ground a few hundred feet south of the pump station, there is the sign. There is also a sign that says, "Do not stand on pipe." I got the pump station supervisor to take my picture standing on the pipe in front of the zero-mile marker sign. I also have a picture standing at the eight-hundred-mile sign in Valdez, where the pipe ends at the Valdez Marine Terminal. I had an office and an apartment there too. I drove an Alyeska Truck, wore Alyeska fire-retardant clothing, wore an Alyeska Badge, lived in their camps and rental properties, and ate their food. At home I have an actual piece of the pipeline, a piece that was used as a test weld.

I've read a lot of books on the pipeline and interviewed at least a hundred employees. It was a neat experience. Suffice it to say, some of my knowledge is accurate and well researched, not hearsay and gossip.

After the injunction that stopped the construction, and while I was working in Houston, the owners of the pipeline instituted an "oil shortage." Some of the partners in the oil companies were Arab oil businessman. That's right—the Saudis were investors too. The management went to its Arab partners and asked them to "turn back the tap". They had an interest in completing the pipeline, and so they gladly complied. People who are old enough to have been alive at this time can tell you about rationing of gas at gas stations. There were lines a city block long, and people were getting into fistfights at gas stations, which made the national news. Where I worked in Texas, the biggest oil-producing state in the nation, there were lines. If you worked for a company, there was a special line for contractors. Basically, we didn't have to wait; we'd drive right up to the pump and fill up. But everyone else had to wait in line. Sometimes stations ran out of gas. If you had an even-numbered plate, you went on Monday, Wednesday, or Friday. Odd-numbered plates went on Tuesday, Thursday, and Saturday. The president and the vice president of the United States signed into legislation an act that made the Trans-Alaska Pipeline a matter of national security. It completely squashed the injunction. This way, people couldn't even think about messing with the pipeline. And it worked—boy, did it work. They stitched in the pipeline like it was a new road, and that was it. Done deal! The point is that nobody noticed. No 'Oil-Gate', no movies, just back to life as usual.

The pipeline was originally designed to pump a million barrels a day. But with the addition of a drag-reduction agent, a complex polymer, they were able to safely operate at 2.5 million barrels a day for about nine years. They maxed out at 2.7 million barrels per day. When they signed the legislation, they added some "trailers." This is special, additional legislation—kind of last-minutes thoughts. On occasion, these trailers are more favors to some company or other entity. One of the trailers required that a shipload of oil, or one tanker a month, had to go to an East Coast refinery. In the event of a war, they wanted to have the government get gas and oil for DC, as well as some military installations. I had the honor of eating dinner with the captain of this tanker in Valdez. Alaskans called Valdez "Val-Disease" after the Exxon tanker spill. Another part of the trailer legislation prevented the oil from being sold to anyone outside of the United States. The US government totally reneged on the oil companies' agreement with the Japanese. This was finally rectified around 2010, thirty-three years after the original agreement! For about eight years, the Trans-Alaska Pipeline provided just short of one-quarter of the US domestic demand of crude oil. Today, they are down to less than one-twentieth of the US demand and only pump half a million barrels a day. This is a result of increases in taxes imposed on the producers.

CHAPTER 6

Distractions and Smoke Screens

Two of magicians' favorite ploys are distractions ("Watch this hand while I do something else with the other hand") and smoke screens. If you are smart, you learn how to get politicians, labor leaders, and the media to do your work for you. It's also cost effective to have someone else do your dirty work. Unfortunately for independent environmental groups, ones outside of the government agencies, they have been manipulated in this way. I roomed with all sorts of PR guys, environmental engineers, and geologists in my twenty-one years in the Alaska oil patch. One of the things I learned was that ANWR was a big smoke screen. Early on, back before any environmental groups were paying attention, exploratory drilling was done by Uncle Sam, as well as the oil companies, in the Arctic National Wildlife Refuge. I worked right on the edge of it. That tended to be where the oil was—right along the edge. Drilling technology has come a long way. We can now drill down two miles and horizontally another ten miles. From an environmental position, this is very good. The oil company mucks up maybe ten acres by building a gravel pad on top of the permafrost. Then they drill down two miles and out in every direction another ten miles. In order to draw out the underground resources from three hundred square miles, they leave a very small footprint. On a drill site that is three hundred feet by one thousand feet, you place the wells ten feet apart and can easily have a hundred wells. One such artificial island, which is eight miles out to sea, is only about four to six acres. It was originally built and run by BP. They sold it to a far less responsible oil company, and I wouldn't consider it a safe place to work anymore. It was in ocean water that was only ten to twenty feet deep. I watched them build the island and then inspected there while they constructed the camp and processing equipment. Initially we drove over fifteen-foot-thick sea ice in four-wheel-drive pickups. Then we used short excursion buses, followed by full-sized, over-the-road, Greyhound-type buses. When the ice melted in the summer, we traveled there in several types of boats. When the ice was thin and near breakup in the spring, we rode there in an amphibious, tracked machine. During breakup, we went by hovercraft and helicopter. There were ten different modes of transportation. Needless to say, this type of facility was expensive to operate.

ANWR, pronounced "An-War," has some oil, but it's green. It could actually stand to sit another ten thousand years to cook and mature. Also, it is in a lousy formation. Some oil occurs in rock, and you can't get it out. Some occurs in sand, and it's too expensive to process and too difficult to get out. And then some is just right, like Goldilocks and the porridge. There are lots of in-between formations that might not be profitable initially, but years later, with the advent of new processes and new technology, they become feasible. This was the case with North Dakota and Bakken crude. Its existence was known for many years, and it was by no means a new oil field. But the technology to extract it and the technology to process it made it prohibitively expensive. Forty years later, with new extraction techniques, new processing techniques, and higher prices, it became practical. ANWR's oil's is not so hot. As one of the geochemists described it to me, "Imagine dropping a bunch of grapes into a five-gallon bucket of concrete. Now, after the concrete has hardened, you drill into it. It costs you $4 million to drill into one of the grapes. But that one grape has only $1 million worth of oil. So you drill into another grape—same thing. Now you've spent $8 million to get $2 million worth of oil. A guy could go broke doing this." That's kind of the case with ANWR. By the time we figure out a way to get it out, and the price is sky high, you'll be able to drill into it from a state away without ever disturbing the wildlife. But for the time being, BP isn't interested. They even made this declaration in their magazine.

Nobody believed them. Labor unions, Alaska politicians, and the media were all looking at the fortune to be made. One bumper sticker in Alaska reads, "God, please let there be another pipeline project ... I promise not to piss it away this time," referring to the fortune they made during the initial construction of the pipeline. And of course, the independent environmental groups didn't buy BP's statement either. It cost big bucks for advertising campaigns and legal footwork. The PR guys from the big oil companies noticed. They are quite willing to let labor unions, the politicians, the media, and the environmentalists duke it out. It keeps them out of BP's hair and ties up lots of their valuable manpower and resources, not the oil company's manpower and resources. In short, the four groups are fighting over a dead issue. And big oil is sitting on the sidelines, laughing. They're not even complicit! If I know about this, then it is more than likely that some of the politicians are also aware of it, which *does* make them complicit. That is why ANWR is a big smoke screen.

> Get out your notebook ... There's more.
> —*All the President's Men*

When they started designing the Alaska Pipeline, TAPS, they initially planned to power the line with natural gas. If you are in the gas and oil business, you usually have plenty of gas. Regardless of what business you are in, if you have a choice of fuels, coal, oil, gasoline, or gas, both propane or natural, you would pick gas. Gas burns clean so that the EPA doesn't bother you. But that's not the primary reason. Any engine, whether gasoline, diesel, or jet, or gas turbine, or even the boilers used to make steam, run better on gas. They also last two and a half times as long. A GE LM 2500 costs about $12 to $15 million to rebuild. It's a jet engine—a big one. A jet engine or gas turbine that will run eight thousand hours on liquid fuel (Jet-A, diesel, JP-4, or kerosene) will usually run closer to twenty thousand hours on gas. Piston engines last two and a half times as long running on Gas. The Maintenance is way less. Gas does not fowl up the heat exchangers in big boilers and you do not need a "Scrubber" for the exhaust like those used in a Coal operation. From a maintenance perspective Gas is king.

It takes a lot of energy to move a million barrels of oil eight hundred miles a day. Of the twelve pump stations, only eleven were actually built and operated. Pumps 1, 3, 4, 6, 8, and 10 each have three Rolls Royce 17,500-horsepower jet engines that power pumps. Two operate, and one is a backup when repairing or replacing the other pump or engine. They run 24-7 almost every day of the year. The remaining pump stations, pumps 2, 7, and 9, each had just two prime movers (RR AVONs) and two pumps, of which they only operated one at a time. I've forgotten what the setup was at pump 12, and pump 5 is a relief station to relieve pressure when the line shuts down. Most of the turbines had digital gauges showing their fuel usage, but there were still a few that were using the old analog meters. They were just like the pumps at a gas station, where little wheels with numbers went around showing tenths, gallons, tens, and hundreds. These fuel consumption meters didn't have a tenths wheel. The gallons wheel was a blur. At sixteen gallons a minute, there is a fairly big fire in one of these engines. On a printout it showed twenty-four thousand gallons per day. This is times fifteen units spread across the eight hundred miles. In addition, there were smaller generating units that heated the offices and ran the man camps and other buildings at each pump station. They used quite a bit of fuel. In the early days of the Prudhoe Bay Oil Field and the Alaska Pipeline, the attitude was, "Fuel? What's fuel? We make fuel!" Gas pumps didn't have meters; fuel was free for contractors, and we left vehicles running all night. It was the Arctic; we had to. However, four hundred thousand gallons of fuel per day isn't free either.

After I worked there, they have converted some of the pump stations to electric. Now, instead of a jet engine running the pump, a jet engine runs a generator. A variable-speed, electric motor runs the pump, but it still uses a bunch of fuel.

CHAPTER 7

Coal and Trains versus Gas and Oil

Alaska sits on lots of coal. It's probably enough coal to power the entire country for fifty to one hundred years. The steam era and the industrial revolution revolved around coal. Alaska has a railroad system that runs from Seward and Anchorage to Fairbanks. It doesn't connect to the lower forty-eight states; it doesn't connect to Canada. Smack dab in the middle sits the largest working coal mine in Alaska, the Usibeli Coal Mine, in Healy, Alaska. Imagine a mouse nibbling on a piece of cheese the size of the great pyramid. That's Alaska's coal industry. And they were there first, before the oil guys. Coal used to power everything in Alaska. In Fairbanks, they had a huge, coal-fired steam plant that made electricity and had steam lines run to some of the nearby homes. For a while, Alaska's military presence outnumbered the residents: there were four hundred thousand Alaskans and six hundred thousand military personnel. All the military bases ran on coal. The coal train delivered a load to Eielson AFB, then a load to Ft. Wainwright, then Fairbanks, and then Clear AFB. Next it went on to Anchorage, then Elmendorf AFB and Ft. Greely. From there, it delivered rail cars full of coal to barges that took the coal to the island military outposts of Dutch Harbor, Adak, and Attu. Then it started over. The train didn't really do enough business to be profitable and eventually fell into bankruptcy. The State of Alaska took it over. Uncle Sam pitched in too, with a $30 million subsidiary each year. Eventually, after thirty years, Uncle Sam told the state of Alaska," If you don't know how to operate the railroad business, you should get out of it," and the government cut their federal subsidy in 2000. Alaska paid for it out of oil tax money.

When they were doing the permitting for the oil pipeline, they went ahead and planned for a gas pipeline to power the twelve pump stations and the VMT. When the coal and train guys realized that Fairbanks, Ft. Wainwright, Eielson AFB, and some other towns and bases along the way would likely be able to run natural gas, it looked like curtains for them. They got the politicians of the time to put the decision in the hands of the Railway Commission so that they could block the building of the gas line. They allowed the gas line to go only to pump stations 1 through 4, about 150 miles, but not beyond Atigun Pass, and certainly nowhere near populated areas. The gas pipeline would have created about as many jobs as would have been lost by the railway and coal, but it would have decreased the cost of electricity and heat, and the cost of living, for a majority of Alaskans. The politicians knew this from the start, but they wanted to keep their voters happy, and by passing the buck to the Railway Commission, it made it appear that they were innocent. As of today, the state of Alaska could have built the gas pipeline themselves, cash out of pocket, maybe twice over for what has been spent on advertising campaigns and studies. They gave $500 million to the Canadians for one study alone. The state is greedy. Officials wanted some foreign country, like Japan, China, or Korea, to commit to a long-term contract, which never happened. Yet the politicians have dangled that carrot in front of labor unions for the last thirty years: "When the gas pipeline comes …"

It hasn't always been in Big Oil's best interest to sell the gas—not yet, anyway. Ideally, you use the gas to get as much oil out of an oil field as you can, and then you sell the gas.

When one initially punches a hole into an oil formation, it is usually under pressure. That pressure will push the product right up to the surface for you … for a while. Then as the pressure plays out, you have to start pumping it. With this technique, all one can expect to recover is about 10 percent; the rest stays trapped in rock and dirt. If you drill a bunch of wells along the outside edge of the formation and then push gas and water back in the ground, you can recover another 10 percent. This is called enhanced recovery. So with enhanced recovery, you can get 20 percent of the oil and these, days you develop a field right from the start with this in mind. This reinjection is not to be confused with fracking. Fracking, from the word fracture, is just that. If you can fracture the formation it will, break up the rock and make trapped oil accessible, and you can get better flow rates. It's done lots of ways. Initially, they used nitro glycerin. They simply dropped it right down the well. Half the guys that performed fracking with nitro glycerin were killed doing it. Later came TNT. It was safer because it could be set off electrically, but it often did so much damage to the well bore that they could not get the pipe back out of the ground to service the well. Sometimes certain chemicals can be applied at great pressure to loosen up the formation. They use crude oil and diesel pumped at very high pressure. One of the problems with fracking is that it is imperative to have a good seal between the formation and shallower water tables. The water tables—of which there are often two, one at 30–100 feet and a second at 100–500 feet—are freshwater. Where you pass through these layers, you need to prevent whatever material you are trying to inject into the oil formation, which is usually several thousand feet deeper, from polluting these upper reservoirs. Failure to do so is criminal in that the damage is potentially dangerous and often permanent. Oil guys don't usually give a damn. It is difficult to see what is going on that deep underground, so it's easy to get away with. It is also possible to not be aware that you are doing it. But ignorance does not equate to innocence. Whether or not you know about it, if you are polluting the water table, you are damaging the environment and creating a toxic hazard.

CHAPTER 8

The Best Job Ever!

The petrochemical industry is probably the highest paying industry in the world for blue-collar workers. It didn't matter what you did; if you did it for petrochemical, it paid more. I had an apprentice, a very bright young man and an Alaska native. We were moving this big man camp—essentially a portable hotel made out of Acco trailers stacked three stories high. This one was a 616-man camp. It had a huge chow hall, massive commercial kitchens, and four massive Laundromats with ten washers and ten dryers in each. There was a sauna and a theater. In both the *Anchorage Daily News* and the *Fairbanks Daily News Miner* were articles that compared Alaska wages to the lower forty-eight states. They had carpenters, painters, plumbers, electricians, cooks, doctors, lawyers, welders, and mechanics. Pretty much across the board, everyone made 20 percent more in Alaska than in the lower forty-eight. They didn't bother to mention that it cost 20 percent more to live in Alaska. At the bottom of the articles in both papers was a disclaimer to the effect of, "This does not include North Slope Oil Workers." Our wages were so out of line with the rest of the world that they didn't include them in the study. My apprentice, Robert, made as much as a doctor in the lower forty-eight, and I made as much as a lawyer. These were the two highest paying positions listed in the study. We were just a couple of electricians. We made triple what "sparkies" in the lower forty-eight made.

A lot of good ol' boys from the oil states (Texas, Louisiana, Arkansas, Mississippi) who were sometimes not even high school grads made $100,000–200,000 a year. You didn't have to be literate; you simply needed good people skills. One's entry ticket into a cushy, high-paying job was the "FBI" system. That translates to **F**riends, **B**rothers, and **I**n-laws—or **F**ull-**B**looded Indian! It wasn't what you knew, but whom you knew.

My observations from working in and around the oil industry from 1976 to 2016 were that it was not really a competitive business. In a competitive business, you have to be fairly consistent, not make too many mistakes, and deliver your product at a reasonable price, or else you will be undercut by the competition and go out of business. I did a lot of bidding and estimating for electrical construction. Bid too high, and someone else gets the job; bid too low, and you lose money. There is a limited margin of error. The exceptions to the rule are businesses that don't have much competition, or ones that are monopolies. The various cartels formed by steel companies, and later by the oil industry, amount to a legitimate monopoly. They can set the price. Take a close look at power companies. They rarely go out of business, they are monopolies, and they are tightly regulated. Oil is not as tightly regulated. An oil company can make a major blunder to the tune of millions, if not billions, and still survive. Most other businesses can't do that and survive. The *Exxon Valdez* incident is a good example. Exxon paid serious fines, footed the bill for an expensive cleanup, and shelled out millions to litigants … but they are still the second biggest oil company in the world. Their net worth exceeds that of many small countries. Granted that they are much better businessmen than almost any politicians.

When I was inspecting on the Trans-Alaska Pipeline, roughly 1.0–1.2 million barrels of crude flowed through it a day. That translated to around $50 million per day. In the time you could tell a good joke, a million dollars flowed by. Likewise, at one of the smaller oil fields I worked at, they produced close to twenty thousand barrels a day, which equated to roughly three-quarters of a billion dollars per year. This was enough to cover the light bill, so to speak. Even though it cost $200 million for maintenance and operation a year, there was still some room for mistakes. I worked on a series of projects with $500 million price tags and payrolls that ran $1 million per week. That was the norm for petrochemical development.

THE COOK'S STORY

I got this story from several North Slope cooks, not just one.

He used to be the head chef at some expensive, top-of-the-line restaurant in New York. He made sixty thousand a year. Then he came up on the pipeline and started making $140,000. He only has to work half the year. (Most of the positions rotate, where one works two weeks on and two weeks off. There's also a four-and-two rotation, and a three-and-three.) In any other job, one was lucky to get a couple of weeks off a year. Here, he got two weeks off every two weeks! At the restaurant, if he wanted something out of the ordinary, he had to whine and cry to get it. Here, he snaps his fingers, and instantly he has five hundred pounds of prime rib or king crab.

You didn't see any skinny North Slope oil workers. They fed us steak, shrimp, lobster, king crab, duck, and salmon. It was too much. You had to go on R & R just to take a break from eating too much! They had a night chef who was also the baker. He made cakes, pies, donuts, cookies, brownies—you name it. The salad bars there were better than most restaurants. There was also a place where one could make one's own sandwiches, with fruit and hot dogs, chili, or some type of soup. It was open 24-7. I had heard that navy guys on submarines ate the best of anybody, but it was hard to beat the chow at the camps in the oil patch.

AWOL ENVIRONMENTALISTS

I briefly worked with this person who was the head of environmental. This person had a PhD in environmental science from a major university and was nice to work with. All the environmental people were nice to work with. We always had permanent, on-site environmental people at the larger sites. Most of them didn't have PhDs, but they did have some degree of education. Normally, anywhere else in the lower-forty-eight, environmental folks that worked for agencies like the EPA, DEC, or DEQE and made minimal wages. Not on the pipeline and on the Prudhoe Bay Oil Field. These people pulled in the real bread, making them the highest paid environmental workers on the planet. The head of environmental made a six-digit income, and it didn't start with a one. After some years, that person was offered a much better paying position with one of the Big Oil companies. They took the position, worked it for some years, and then went back to their original position. AWOL, with pay!

CHAPTER 9

The Pipeline

In 1992, when I was still working for Boeing outside of Seattle, some inspectors on the Alaska Pipeline were complaining about some unsafe equipment at the Valdez Marine Terminal. It's right on the ocean, and if you are even near saltwater, corrosion happens. One of their sparkies got shocked. They whined and complained, and the pipeline ran them all off. One of the parties got hooked up with an attorney. The attorney got in touch with some news reporter from a newspaper back east—one usually associated with the stock market. The writer, who didn't know anything about petrochemical, had never been to Alaska and didn't know squat about electrical. He generated this bogus article and painted a picture of the pipeline that suggested the Trans -Alaska Pipeline was Chernobyl, about to blow off the face of the planet and take Alaska with it. Unlike the *Washington Post,* which checked their sources and verified facts that were about to go to press, this reporter didn't.

The next thing you know, it's on CNN and in *Time* magazine. But they didn't check sources either, they just said "according to ..." If it ever makes it on to UPI or AP, that's pretty much it. They are just a wire service, and under freedom of speech, they can pretty much say or write whatever they want, whether it's true or false. A watchdog agency of seventeen federal and state agencies oversee the pipeline, some of which are the National Forest Service, the National Wildlife Service, the Alaska Department of

Labor, the Federal Department of Labor, and the EPA. I used to be pretty good at reciting them all. They are all grouped together into a single office called the Joint Pipeline Office (JPO). I worked with the JPO. One of my old tool partners switched over to them for a while. Because the JPO includes so many federal agencies, they have to answer to Congress. When the safety issues at the pipeline started to flare up courtesy of the bogus articles in the media, Congress told the parent oil companies to deal with it.

The oil companies said, "Sure, we'll get right on it," and they did. They hired about four hundred people and went through the pipeline with a fine-tooth comb. In June of 1994, I was sworn in as an electrical inspector on the Trans-Alaska Pipeline. That fifty dollars I got swindled out of in Houston in 1977 was paid back with interest on the first day! About four years into my stretch with the pipeline, I often was the one who showed new employees the ropes; it was a bit like being a tour guide. The Alaska Pipeline is very strict; they live and abide by policy and rules. You don't go anywhere or do anything without permission from the operator, a permit, and all the proper personal protective equipment. It's enough procedural stuff that people go through a bunch of training before they ever set foot on one of the facilities, even guests.

I used to grill the employees who had been there since they'd built the place. I pored over the drawings, asked more questions, and left no stone unturned. I inspected inside and outside every facility on the pipeline.

Out of a workforce of three thousand, I only met one or two people who got their jobs for the oil companies because of their credentials. Everybody else came in through the "FBI" door. The subcontractor I worked for was extremely well organized. The owner, whom I went out of my way to meet, was a real man of his word and was almost a saint. Honesty and integrity were his way of life. Unfortunately, many oil workers, including many of his employees, didn't know what those words meant. But being well funded always smoothed things out. If you ran out of Sheetrock tape, you could always patch the hole with hundred-dollar bills.

They paid our transportation to and from work from the point of hire, so it didn't matter where we lived. Fully half of the workforce was from the lower forty-eight; originally, it was more like 90 percent. The Alaskans got fed up with the Texans, and some Texans moved to Alaska and became Alaskans. After they completed and started up the pipeline, a popular bumper sticker read, "Happiness is a Texan with an Oakey on each arm ... going home!"

Boeing took safety seriously, but Alyeska took safety to a much higher level. Initially we went through five days of training: listen to the instructor, watch a video, take a test, repeat, for ten hours a day—for which we were paid handsomely. They drug-tested us; checked our hearing, eyes, and respiratory fitness; gave full physicals; and then flew us to Fairbanks for a further week of safety training. For my position, one had to have previous experience as an inspector, an inspection certificate, and master electrician licenses in at least two states. They ran us through their own inspection certification program and had us take and pass the Alaska electrical certificate of fitness exam. It's essentially Alaska's Journeyman Electrician certification. We were fitted with gas masks and sprayed with pepper gas. All this before we ever set foot on a pump station! At every site, like a pump station, the VMT, or other oil processing facility, there was some additional safety training unique to that site: where to go in an emergency, which radio channel to use, permitting requirements—that kind of stuff. We never went anywhere without our FRCs, hard hat, safety glasses, radios, and sometimes a Scott Air Pack. They were more stringent than most military operations I had visited. In the petrochemical racket, you don't do anything without a permit. They had an entire rainbow of colors of specialty permits. For some jobs, you need two or three, and they may require verification and review by everyone, including the Queen of England. For lots of the training, such as the training for the permitting process, we took it every year once we signed on.

I had previously worked on some electrical construction jobs for a couple of consecutive weeks of twelve-hour days, and I questioned whether I could do this. At the end of two weeks of twelve-hour days, I hardly knew which end was up. And this was going to be a four-and-two rotation, so twenty-eight consecutive twelve-hour days. It turned out to be easy. There was no commute; I was already at work. I didn't have to shop or cook; they fed me. They even made my bed once a week.

After I realized I could handle the long hours, I started working longer hitches: eight weeks, then nine weeks. Eventually I ended up doing an eighteen-week hitch, took ten days off, and did a nineteen-week hitch. All of this was in dark, subzero conditions. We got weeks of thirty and forty degrees below zero. The lowest ambient I experienced was sixty-six below, at Galbraith Lake. That was the ambient—wind chills got lower.

The Arctic storms were exhilarating. Four to six times a year, we would get a blow that had winds that hit force eleven on the Beaufort Scale—that's hurricane-force winds. It rattled the buildings and sand-blasted decals and lettering off signs. The BP, Alaska, and American flags in front of the camp had to be replaced fairly frequently. There were three "phase" conditions. Phase one was nasty, but we could still get around. Phase two was pretty serious; convoy only, usually escorted by a Road Grader in front and a Loader in back. Phase three was the real stuff—zero visibility. While sitting in the cab of a crew-cab, four-wheel-drive, three-quarter-ton truck, which was about the only thing we drove, we couldn't see the hood of the truck. We usually had to stay in the camp, but on occasion workers got stranded outside and had to spend the night in their truck or at one of the processing facilities. Blows usually didn't last many days, but it took another day or two to get dug out and get back to work.

As inspectors, we documented everything. The rule of thumb in the inspection racket is if it's not documented, it didn't happen. When I witnessed tests, the form I used required multiple signatures, instruments had to have current and valid calibration dates, every *T* had to be crossed, and every *I* was dotted. We went through a special course just for making corrections. Everything got checked, rechecked, and checked again. There were three tiers of inspection. We cut down an entire forest for the paper used to document changing a light bulb. If someone tried to cover something up, heads would roll. They would fire the foreman, the safety people, the craft hands, and anyone involved. Trying to hide any mistake meant losing your high-paying job and probably not getting invited back. It was their playpen, and you did what they said do. Get in a fight? There goes your badge! You're out. The reality of how and what we did was 180 degrees from what is portrayed by the media and movie industry, or what many environmental folks believed was going on. I kept daily reports for every day I was there. A lot of environmentalists would be grossly disappointed by my daily reports because none of the type of stuff they assume the oil companies were doing happened. We had special explosion-proof cameras that were approved to be used in hazardous areas, such as where there was oil and gas. We always took pictures. If a loader broke a hydraulic hose, we took pictures. The environmental guy came along with the safety guy, and we documented it and cleaned it up.

The most ironic part was that the big companies, the ones always portrayed in movies—BP, Arco, Phillips, Conoco, Mobile Exxon—were the ones that came closest to playing by the rules. It was the smaller companies, the very ones the environmentalists ignored, that broke the rules. The smaller guys had the most spills, most fires, and most accidents, and they did cover them up. Big outfits like BP could afford to have all the staffing available for safety people, safety engineers, and six different kinds of inspectors, including environmental. Smaller companies couldn't afford full-time environmental people, and they couldn't afford safety people and inspectors. They did hide and cover up stuff. One has to maintain the frame of reference here, which is, "This is Alaska." In other countries, and especially offshore, all bets are off. Even oil development sites in the lower forty-eight were not in the league of how clean an operation they ran in Alaska. Perhaps the second cleanest oil operation in the world is in the North Sea, between England, Scotland, and Ireland and Norway, Denmark, and Sweden. It's a big fishing ground for the Scandinavians. Oil workers who had worked in the North Sea would substantiate that their operation wasn't quite as up to snuff as Alaska's, as far as cleanliness went.

On an offshore rig, even the ones in US waters, the "tool pusher," or just "pusher" is the main person in control. In international waters, outside of the US territorial waters, the tool-pusher is like the captain of a ship. Maritime law kicks in, so they can get away with a lot. "Safety? Who needs it. This is my ship! You do what I say, or we might just toss you over the side! And we definitely are not having any damn inspectors here!" Consequently they are very dangerous and are quite an environmental threat. In the Gulf alone, there had been one thousand fires and explosions on offshore rigs and platforms before the *Deepwater Horizon* blew out. If you look it up, there is a list of the top one hundred oil spills in just the last fifty years. On that list, the *Exxon Valdez* is not even in the top twenty.

Historically, the largest spill in history took place in the Gulf, off the coast of Mexico. That was the I-TOX 1 spill. It happened in 1977, when I was working in Houston. Years later, I had a friend and roommate who had been an underwater welder and diver. He worked on trying to plug the I-TOX-1 well blowout. He had framed photos. It made the shoreline black with heavy crude from the US-Mexico border all the way around to Miami. After a couple of hurricanes it pretty much dispersed.

CHAPTER 10

Mud

It's all about the mud. Mud is a mixture of water and some fine powder that is used in the drilling process. It serves a multitude of purposes. Initially, it acts like cutting-oil that machinists would use when drilling, cutting, turning, or milling a piece of metal. It gets pumped down through the drill pipe at incredibly high pressure; this lubricates and cools the bit. It also pushes all the tailings, or cuttings, back up to the surface. By analyzing the mud with the tailings in it, you can map what materials you are drilling through. If you start finding coal, copper, silver, gold, or uranium, you chart it so that later you can go back and mine that out. Also, if you drill through something too hard that would destroy the bit, you can know how much pressure to put on the drill bit the next time you punch into that formation. The hole, usually about a foot in diameter, can be anywhere from two to ten miles. The mud coming up around the outside of the pipe acts as lubricant. Mud is also used for directional control. By controlling the mud pressure very carefully, you can curve the drill around. If you have good enough seismic surveying equipment and its associated electronics, you can drill horizontally into the layer where the oil is located.

One of the most important functions of mud is blowout control. When one initially taps into a new formation, it is often under a great deal of pressure that can exceed 10,000 psi. The column of mud can hold down the immense pressure. Imagine holding a glass of water at arm's length. Now imagine trying to hold a thousand glasses of water, one stacked upon the other. It would be pretty heavy. That's how you hold down the pressure if you want to screw on another piece of pipe. But sometimes water is not heavy enough, and so you lace it with something like marble dust to increase its specific gravity. Stones usually sink in water because they are heavier than water. The chemicals used to make mud for oil drilling contain expensive minerals. It usually comes in bags like concrete. Drilling a new well can use several tanker trucks full of mud. It all depends on the depth or length of the hole and the diameter. As you go deeper, you increase the size. Because mud is expensive, you try to reuse as much as possible. On the rig, there will be some shaker screens to remove the tailings so that you can reuse at least part of the mud. Most blowouts occur because they don't use heavy-enough mud. A bubble of gas pushes its way past the mud, and now you have 10,000 psi at the top of the well. Hoses explode, seals give out, and *bang*—you have a big problem. How are you going to plug it up? What if it catches on fire? Yeah. Until Red Adair, the famous oil well fire fighter, came along, no one knew how to put out an oil well fire or even a blowout that didn't catch fire. In some cases, fires burned for years.

Drilling is usually performed by specialty drilling contractors with names like Doyan, Nabors, Parker, and Halliburton. The client (Shell, Exxon Mobile, or BP) hires one of the drilling companies. A representative of the client is usually the second-in-command at an exploratory drill rig. The company man, the tool pusher, and the mud man were arguing about the mixture when the *Deepwater Horizon* blew up. That's the way it usually happens. Things get a bit more complicated when you are drilling in water a mile deep.

Mud men have a really inglorious title. But in reality, many of them are college-educated geochemists who have been to additional mud-training schools. Often they know as much or more about a well than anyone else on the rig.

CHAPTER 11

Expensive False Report

It was surprising how phony and outright dishonest the media was when it came to reporting stuff about the pipeline and the oil patch. This is one example. One afternoon in the summer, I had just completed some inspection work at a facility called Endicott. It was a smaller operation that sat on a sliver of land that was essentially an island with a sand causeway to access it. It was a full sixty miles from my home base, another small operation. I was passing through the two biggest operations, the Eastern Operating Area and the Western Operating Area. These were the biggest oil fields in North America. Each one had three processing facilities and had exceeded a-million-barrels-a-day production for many years. As an inspector in a BP truck, I had pretty much free run of the place. Just like everyone else there, I still had to check in with security and get entry clearance from the area operator, but I was usually exempted from having a permit.

At one place, I passed a bunch of trucks and security personnel. Something was going on! It was a nice sunny summer day, warm with mosquitoes biting. The tundra was green. All the BP guys and the security guys were standing around this little eight- or ten-inch pipe. It was a produced water line, and it had sprung a leak. Produced water is the water that comes up with the oil, and it is separated out and removed. It may still contain 5–10 percent oil, but it's usually fairly clear. I wouldn't drink it, but it definitely isn't oil; it simply has some trace amounts in it. It generally it gets reinjected back into the formation.

The leak had been caught right away and shut off. It left a small brown spot on the green tundra about the size of a five-gallon bucket, not much more than a foot across. There are teams of workers constantly inspecting pipes for corrosion. They take x-rays and run little robots called "Pig's", through the pipes that take microwave pictures and ultrasound pictures of the inside of the pipe. The pictures go to specialty engineers who review them and look for potential failure spots. If a pipe has an initial thickness of a quarter inch and one-thirtieth of an inch corrodes away, it's fairly easy for the corrosion engineers to predict when that pipe will fail. One goes in well before that time and repairs or replaces it. The pipe has various corrosion protections on the outside, such as thick epoxy paint or special thick gooey tape. Over the corrosion protection is placed two to six inches of a hard thermal insulation, usually some form of Styrofoam or Urethane. Over that is a thin tin or aluminum outer sheath.

A team of insulators had been instructed to remove some insulation for the x-ray guys. As they were taking the insulation off the line, it started leaking. Practically every worker in the Prudhoe Bay Oil Field carries a two-way radio. They are very specialized, expensive radios that are specifically designed to work in hazardous environments. An explosion-proof, class-one, division-one radio costs about $3,000. You could use it while taking a shower in gasoline, and it would not ignite the gas, guaranteed! Almost every truck has a radio too. The insulators called in the leak right away, the line was shut down, and maybe thirty to fifty gallons of the produced water drained onto the tundra through a pencil-sized hole. I was there—that's what really happened.

But when I got back to my camp, that was not what they reported on the major network new stations—all of them! Back at my home facility, the chow hall is like a sports bar. It has four giant TVs that are on 24-7. All the news media throughout North America claimed, "They shut down the Alaska Pipeline." That never happened. The massive forty-eight-inch Alaska Pipeline didn't even have a hiccup. All that got shut down was this small produced water line that ran from one of the gathering centers to another gathering center. On TV they showed some pictures of an oil spill, a real bad crude leak, from two years earlier, but it was in the winter, and the black crude really showed up on the white snow. That crude oil leak covered an area about fifty to one hundred square feet—an area bigger than my crew cab truck. What's more, all the guys standing around were wearing Arctic parkas. They didn't bother to put in any type of disclaimer stating that this was file footage or indicating that these were not actual pictures of the leak.

As I'm munching down my dinner, a coworker points out the fact that in all the pictures on TV, the guys are wearing their Arctic gear. It was the middle of the summer! I was there an hour ago, and there wasn't any crude. What were they trying to pull here? The next morning, the price of oil on the stock market went up a nickel as a result of the false report. Gas stations in turn raised their price a nickel, and you paid a nickel a gallon more for your gas. That false report cost Americans about $100 million in anticipation of a break in the supply chain that never took place. False reporting by the media!

The line-wide inspection of the Trans-Alaska Pipeline that resulted from bogus reporting cost $345 million, but we didn't find very much wrong. I made a point of asking about sixty of the eighty electrical inspectors I worked with on that project, "What do you think about the pipeline?" Almost everyone's response was something like "This is the best installation I'd ever seen." It was. Alyeska ran a tight ship. Their pipeline was spotlessly clean and painted. You could eat off the floor of the pump room or anywhere else. It didn't leak anywhere. On the rare occasion where a guy planted an explosive charge on the pipe and blew a hole in it, they fixed it and cleaned up the spot, and one couldn't tell it ever happened. In another case, when some Alaskan did not like the pipeline, he shot at it with a high-power rifle, and after several shots he managed to punch a small hole in it. They spotted it right away, shut it down, fixed it, cleaned up the area, and went right back to work. The Alaska pipeline, in its entire history of almost forty years, transporting over twenty billion barrels, has leaked less fuel than consumers drop at the pumps in one state, in one year. But that fact, which is technically accurate, is not the picture painted by the media, and it's not what most environmentalists would believe. People tend to believe what they want to, not necessarily the truth. Most of those same inspectors whom I had asked their opinions were not all that anxious to make a public statement attesting to the safety and security of the pipeline, primarily because it was the best-paying job they ever had, and they would tell you that. Up until that time, it was the best job I'd ever had.

Many people reading this account might jump to the conclusion that I was pro oil and anti-environmentalist. They would be dead wrong. What you've been led to believe isn't always correct. I was there; the newspapers were not there. No TV camera crews or reporters were there. And an appalling amount of the reporting was incorrect. It was sensationalism and hype, inflating stories to get folks to pay attention. That's the way of life with the media. They are trying to sell a product. Some reporters are just trying to make names for themselves. If you want truth, look at a scientific journal like *Physics Today* or *Scientific American* because they don't sell *stories*. If they print something that is the slightest bit incorrect, they immediately get corrected by the entire scientific community. Science is usually not about politics. Generally, with some limited exceptions, they are not trying to sell a product. They are exploring the truth about how things work.

The big companies do not always go out of their way to hide stuff. They figure it's better to pay the fine and not open themselves up to a bunch of hearsay. They have tons of PR guys and gals. I had one as a roommate at one of the oil camps. He tipped me off about one of the diversions I'm writing about. Environmental extremists cook up all sorts of conspiracy theories, but they are usually not based on actual reporting. It would be natural to assume that the oil companies were trying to hide something because of how tight their security is. Generally, you do not get on to a petrochemical facility unless you belong there. The big oil companies have several legitimate reasons for this. They have hundreds of millions to hundreds of billions of dollars at stake. There are a lot of hazards there too. High pressure, flammability, toxicity, and large amounts of energy are among the top contenders. They put you through all sorts of safety training, and there are still accidents. Think about it. You have a gas compressor that is compressing gas to 3,500 psi, at a massive volume, in the millions of cubic feet a day, and it's driven by some massive turbine, engine, or motor. The gas is combustible, bordering on explosive, and may contain some toxic ingredients. Which part of *dangerous* didn't you get? And the last thing you need is some guy lighting up anywhere nearby. It becomes irrelevant whether it's pot, cigarettes, or a vaporizer. You also don't want someone who is drunk or stoned operating that equipment. And you have to keep out terrorists, would-be saboteurs, and anyone who doesn't belong. Hell, even the guy's that belong there, who are not drunk, or stoned, who have been trained screw up. Petrochemical facilities are just an inherently dangerous place. If you don't belong there, you shouldn't be there. Your putting people and equipment at unnecessary risk.

Contrary to public opinion, BP would routinely allow non-governmental groups to tour their facilities. They would run Greenpeace guy's through $10,000 to $20,000 worth of safety training per person, suit them up in expensive fire-retardant outfits, and provide them with a bus and a guide. Then they would take them wherever they wanted to go and let them see nearly everything. They would even room with us in the camps and eat with us in the chow hall. From talking with them, it was obvious that they still thought we were hiding something. Many had clearly been brainwashed by the movies and media. Smaller outfits can't afford this approach and don't offer the tours very often.

It's like I said earlier: if you really want to know what is going on, go to work there and get a firsthand look.

SPILLS? CLEAN IT UP, PAY THE FINE, GO BACK TO WORK

At one of the remote sites out on the pipeline, there was a ten-thousand-gallon underground propane tank. It was at a location that you could get to only in the summer, and it got filled up once a year. The tank was grossly oversized. They had overestimated how much fuel would be used in a year. One spring the gas tank driver topped off the tank. Later that year, a maintenance technician for Alyeska checked the level gauge on the tank, and it was empty. He reported it, and there was a big investigation. Alyeska paid some big fine. They couldn't find the leak. Back

comes the gas tank truck. Yet he can't squeeze in but a few gallons
of gas. The gauge was broken! There was no leak! No one went
back and corrected the records. Alyeska didn't try to get the fine
back; they simply went about their business. But the records still
show that they had a big spill that never really happened. It gave
the environmentalists something to complain about.

Because the Alaska Pipeline was not allowed to build the
gas pipeline the entire eight hundred miles of the Trans-Alaska
Pipeline, they had to revise their design. To power pump stations
5 through 12, they built three topping units. These are essentially
mini refineries that take crude out of the pipeline and make jet
engine fuel. They put one at pump 6 that could supply pumps 5
through 8, one at pump 8 that could supply the entire line, and
one at pump 10 that could supply pumps 8 through 12. Due to this
modification of the original design, tandem trailer tankers had to
transport fuel up and down the line from the topping units to the
stations that couldn't make their own fuel. Transporting fuel by
truck is inherently more hazardous than by pipeline. Trains and
trucks wreck and spill more oil than a pipeline will lose in a leak
situation; this has been well documented, and a recent scenario
demonstrates this. Bakken crude that is being trucked and trans-
ported by rail to Canadian Refineries has already spilled more
crude in just a few years than most pipelines do in their entire
service lives. In one case, a trainload of crude wiped an entire
Canadian town right off the map in a massive derailment.

It takes more energy to haul any product by rail or truck than it
does by pipeline. More fuel gets used, and that in turn creates more
pollution. More gets spilled by rail and road. I think I'd opt out for
a pipeline, given the alternatives. There's less pollution, and they're
safer and more efficient, which equates to less by-product pollution.

CHAPTER 12

The River of Coal

Worldwide, we burn a lot of coal. Coal is abundant and cheap, but it does not burn cleanly. Regardless of this, coal probably still produces more of the world's electricity than any other fuel source. If one flies over the corners of Wheeling, West Virginia; Pittsburg, Pennsylvania; and Fleshing, Ohio, it looks like the whole world is coal. The Ohio part is called Egypt Valley. This is one of the United States' biggest coal-generating areas. From there, coal trains take the coal to power plants all over the East Coast. Some are dedicated coal trains that service one coal-fired power plant. They make a trip every day, every other day, or every three days to a coal-fired power plant, and then they go back and get another load. They are usually eighty to one hundred cars long, and each car holds 100–120 tons of coal.

The trains that cross over the Appalachian Mountains go through a famous railway pass, perhaps the busiest railroad pass in North America. Altoona has an interesting, winding rail bed that winds its way up and over the Appalachians. In order to gain altitude, there is a place where rail cars going one direction pass cars going the opposite direction, and they are all part of the same train. Instead of just one rail line, there are several side by side. It's also the site of some serious wrecks. From an airplane, it looks like a river of coal leaving Egypt Valley, going up over the mountains, and then heading back down the other side to several ocean port loading facilities to be loaded on ships and barges. On the East Coast side, there are rail yards that have one hundred sets of tracks fanning out side by side to store the trains while they are waiting to load on the ships. It resembles the alluvial fan, where a river deltas out into the ocean. But it's not water—it's coal. Other places in other countries are doing the exact same thing. They have their own little (and often big) rivers of coal flowing from mines to power-generation facilities. China is the biggest user currently. On a worldwide basis, the river is probably roughly half the size of the Mississippi River. Most of the people who don't believe man is playing a part in global warming overlook this fact. This river burns nonstop 24 hours a day, 365 days a year.

If I light a match, it has a limited effect worldwide, but it does have an effect. There are those who think it's insignificant. Those people generally have no understanding of the laws of thermodynamics or the laws of physics. One match affects the entire planet. If a million people each light a match, it has a million times the effect. Historical data indicates that volcanic eruptions have affected the weather. When Krakatoa erupted, it put enough ash in the atmosphere to ring the earth twice. This resulted in no summer the following year. Crops didn't come in, people all over the planet starved, and it snowed in June in New England.

Besides the river of coal being burned, there is a similar river of oil being burned. Granted that it's not quite as big, but it's still quite big. The United States uses about twenty million barrels a day. China uses more than that. Every country, and most islands, are continuously burning fuel. The total is staggering, and it amounts to a big fire. The combination of oil and coal is in the order of some volcanoes, but it's continuous. This is definitely going to affect the planet. The person who publicly denounces these truths is a bit like a dunce waving a flag that says, "Hey, look at me. I'm an Idiot, I'm blind, and I don't have a clue. I'm not very observant." I definitely have not taken a look at the big overall picture.

CHAPTER 13

Diesel-Gate

So what's the story here? Gasoline engines have compressions levels that range between 4:1 and 10:1. That's a ratio of how much the pistons squeeze down the oxygen/fuel mixture before it explodes. Diesels run much higher compression levels, ranging from 18:1 to 24:1. As it turns out there, is more energy, pound for pound and gallon for gallon, in diesel than there is in gasoline. To see how much actual energy there is in a material, such as gun powder, kerosene, gasoline, diesel, wood, or coal, one measures out a small quantity—say, a gram—burns it, and counts the calories of energy released. Surprisingly, gasoline has more energy than gun powder. But diesel has even more.

Due to its high compression level, the diesel engine burns that fuel more efficiently and more completely. The emissions from a diesel are carbon, carbon dioxide, and water. The carbon dioxide definitely adds to greenhouse gas. But the carbon and the water are both nontoxic and biodegradable. That nasty-looking black smoke you see coming out of the city bus is mostly these three components. Gasoline engines, on the other hand, generate all sorts of more toxic, not-so-biodegradable gasses, like carbon monoxide and CO_3. Carbon monoxide (CO), is really bad. You can't see it, but it's deadly. We do all kinds of things to try to eliminate it. That's what catalytic converters on gasoline engines are for: to burn up all the incompletely burned gasses. In a horsepower-to-horsepower, pound-per-pound comparison of diesels to gasoline, the diesel uses about 20–25 percent less fuel to make the same horsepower. Therefore it produces 20–25 percent less carbon, carbon dioxide, and emissions. Many people assume that the black stuff from the diesel is worse than the invisible stuff from the gasoline engine. As it turns out, the opposite is true. The gasoline engine is not only producing much more deadly fumes, but it's producing a larger quantity.

Diesels got exempted from emissions testing for a long time. Once they are worn out or out of adjustment they pollute. But a Tandem Tractor Trailer, being pulled by a big Kenworth or Volvo Tractor with at Cat or Cummings engine that only has 200,000 miles on it would produce less pollution than the 7 to 11 Automobiles that would be burning the equivalent fuel.

Subaru recently designed and built a four-cylinder diesel for the American market. It was designed to meet or exceed the current and future emission standards of all states, including California. The Japanese have more stringent standards than the United States. Someone, somewhere, convinced Subaru to *not* import them. It had nothing to do with meeting any American safety or emissions standards. They have been selling like hot cakes in countries like Australia.

The Volkswagens that have the little four-cylinder, two-liter engines and are being recalled happened to be one of the single most fuel-efficient vehicles ever produced. Only electrics like the Tesla, and hybrids like the Prius, exceed the VW TDI in fuel efficiency. Because of this high efficiency, one of these cars will use less fuel in its lifetime than almost any other automobile currently in production. Most important, those cars will produce less carbon dioxide than any other car produced around the same time. If you take all those cars out of service and replace them with anything but a hybrid or electric, which is not happening currently, the replacements are going to generate more pollution. How did this happen? Emissions are measured in tons. Almost any substitute for the VW TDI will generate at least an additional ton of emissions over the course of its lifetime. Now, multiply this by half a million vehicles. What happened?

FOLLOW THE MONEY

There are five distinct parties that have an interest in seeing this happen. They have a monetary interest in crushing VW and Subaru.

First and foremost is other car companies, especially domestic ones like Ford, Chrysler, and GM. If you don't buy a Subaru or a VW, you might buy an American car. *Might* is the operative word.

The labor unions also have a monetary interest. It's jobs for them.

Third is the oil companies, because you'll have to buy more fuel. But they already have such a strong market that there is limited incentive. Not much motive here.

The fourth and fifth parties are the federal government and the independent state governments. The federal government gets a tax on fuel for every drop you buy. The individual states also impose fuel taxes. If you buy and use more fuel, they take in more taxes. It is not in their best interest to reduce fuel usage. Recently, as the price of fuel was low, some states increased their fuel taxes. The idea was that fewer people would notice and complain. When the price is already higher, it is more difficult to push through legislation to increase the tax without folks noticing. In some sense, that constitutes a conspiracy to defraud the taxpayer in a roundabout way. It definitely constitutes premeditation.

It might be prudent to note that none of these five parties have much of a vested interest in how clean the air we breathe is.

And who did these five guys get to do their dirty work? Some environmental inspectors in California, and the media—thousands of Americans, from inspectors and lab technicians to TV reporters and journalists. A majority of these people probably believe that they are doing the right thing for the environment, but they are being duped and used.

Environmental groups may have had a hand in this, but it is far more likely that they were used to get the ball rolling, so to speak. It would be hard to prove in a court of law, but it's been done before, and people got away with it.

Automobile manufacturers have been known to do some pretty unethical things in the past. They made a concerted effort to eliminate trains. When automobile and truck production was on the rise, and railroads had become complacent, the automobile manufacturers bought up transit systems and shut them down. They got caught and were taken to court. One of the Big Three paid a $55,000 fine. Another of the Big Three paid maybe $10,000. But the damage was done, and it was permanent. Once the infrastructure was gone, it became almost impossible to reestablish it. A train hauls something like six times as much freight for the same amount of fuel that a truck does. That means one-sixth of the pollution. Public transit produces a fractional amount of the pollution to move more people than cars do. This is not my opinion—it's a provable fact. At the end of World War II, Europe was all bombed out. People could not afford new cars, and so they put their efforts toward rebuilding the public transit systems. In many places in Europe, they have some of the best public transit systems in the world, mostly by accident. Here in the United States, there is good to excellent public transit in Boston, New York, Chicago, and Philadelphia. A few other metropolitan areas are starting to catch up, like Portland and some places in California. In Boston, there are not too many places that are not within a few blocks of a bus or train that operates regularly. It sure saves on parking hassles.

CHAPTER 14

Electric Cars

The heart of an electric car is the electric motor. It is quite simple and inexpensive to build, and it lasts significantly longer than any type of reciprocating engine. There's a rotor, two end bearings, and an outer winding. DC motors had brushes that needed regular attention, so that was a source of problems. Also, speed control relative to torque was a problem. After the invention of the semiconductor, like transistors and SCRs, it became possible to eliminate the brushes. Electric motors became ultra-powerful and had so few moving parts that their useful life was roughly ten to twenty times that of any reciprocating engine. They also have superior performance. Gasoline and diesel engines have hundreds of moving parts. There are a lot of frictional parts. The rings on the pistons slide against the cylinder wall, and the cam followers rub against the camshaft. Besides requiring regular oil changes, the rings, pistons, camshaft, and valves all wear out and need to be replaced. For automotive applications, their life is usually limited to ten thousand hours before a major overhaul is required. An electric motor will last one hundred thousand hours. You replace the two end bearings, and it's good for another one hundred thousand hours. It requires nearly no servicing.

If electric motors are cheaper to build, last ten times as long, require no servicing, and have both superior torque (for "jack rabbit" or drag racer starts, and Superior top ends (maximum speeds), why are we not using them? The answer to that is energy storage. Lack of a good battery has always been the Achilles' heel of solar, wind, and electric cars. No battery, no go.

Electric cars started out early. When they first were developing gasoline cars and trucks around 1890, in New York City there were more electric vehicles registered than gasoline. There are some great pictures of rows of hundreds of two-ton Baker Electric Delivery trucks parked in the business districts of New York. Mr. Porsche, the great automobile designer, won a hill climb in 1914 in a four-wheel-drive hybrid with electric motors in the wheels. It got its power from a small gasoline engine that powered a generator. It was basically a wagon with a motor built in to each wheel. In the 1960s, an American engineer, designer, and inventor named Robert G. Letourneau refined and perfected the in-wheel electric wheel drive. He also invented the Earth Mover and promoted the development of giant tires used on big mining equipment. The first Bigfoot, a monster truck, used tires cannibalized off one of Letourneau's giant machines. Numerous automotive manufacturers in Britain, Germany, the United States, and Japan experimented with variations of electric vehicles in the sixties. They would remove the gasoline or diesel engine, the differential, and the transmission, and they'd replace it with some form of electric drive—a combination of a smaller engine running a generator and batteries. A further refinement involved reclaiming the energy lost in breaking. If one uses the electric wheel drives in reverse as generators when they are stopping, it is possible to reclaim 70 percent of the energy it took to get the car, bus, or truck going in the first place. This process is referred to as dynamic regenerative braking. Trains have been using it for many years. It has the significant advantage that unlike brakes, which are hard surfaces grinding away on other hard surfaces, there are no parts that wear out. It's magnetic fields rubbing against magnetic fields. As an electric brake, a motor or generator can last indefinitely. Magnetic fields don't wear. Up until a certain year fairly recently, car, truck, and train brakes were made of asbestos. As the brakes wore down, it put fine asbestos powder in the air. The entire planet was getting asbestos poisoning. For millions of people who have died from lung cancer or liver cancer, some percentage can be blamed on asbestos from brakes. In some countries, they now prohibit asbestos brakes.

Conspiracy theorists falsely jump to the conclusion that the development of electric vehicles would spell doom for the oil companies. Probably not. You will still need the plastics for an electrical insulator, the lubricants, the rubber for tires, and the asphalt for roads. You also still need some type of fuel to make the electricity.

If you take a gallon of gasoline and burn it in a car, it has an overall efficiency of about 20 percent. If you burn that same gallon of gas in a massive Rolls Royce or GE turbine, you can get more like 40–50 percent of the energy. That also means that for a given amount of energy, you will only produce half the pollution to get the same amount of energy. So electric cars don't really threaten the Big Oil guys. But they *do* threaten some of the in-between industries.

It all revolves around the battery. Once someone comes up with a battery that has the same energy power to weight ratio found in liquid fuels like gasoline and diesel, the electric vehicle will make the current technology obsolete overnight. It happened once in history already. One of the defining moments in the Industrial Revolution was the development of the steam engine. This led to steam trains. Steam trains ruled from 1840 to 1940. Then someone designed the diesel electric locomotive. They couldn't scrap out the steam locomotives fast enough. In just a ten- or twenty-year period, almost all the steam engines ever built were scrapped. Why?

Because a steam engine required servicing every three thousand miles, whereas a diesel electric locomotive required servicing every one hundred thousand miles. The real death blow had to do with fuel consumption. Diesel electrics used one-third the fuel. Owners of railroads liked having to do less maintenance and having to only buy one-third the fuel. So did their stockholders.

The development of a good battery will lead to its own industrial revolution. Let's look at what will come and what will go. Gasoline and diesel engine production will cease. Gas stations will close. Major retooling takes place worldwide. How many makes of automobiles can you name? I can name about forty. Motorcycles? At least a dozen makes. All those companies have to retool and re-design. The new technology creates as many jobs as it takes away, but some will have to learn the new technology. If you are reading this, you may live to see them close the emissions testing stations. There will be a lot of building new power lines and power infra-structure; it's already in the works. Engineers are planning ahead for how much the power grid is going to have to be built up. It is currently not big enough to handle a rapid increase in load to charge millions of cars at home.

Huge power lines running east to west across the nation will shore up the aging grid. This will allow surplus wind and solar from the east to power the west, and vice versa. As New York goes to sleep, California can be using their surplus. Wind power generated at three in the morning in California can be shuttled to and used by East Coasters while West Coasters are still sleeping and don't need it. It will also be charging electric cars.

One of the things done during the Depression to get things back going were these huge work projects. They built bridges, roads, dams, and power production facilities, and it worked. The most notable of these WPA and CCC projects were Grand Coulee

Dam, and the Tennessee Valley Authority. It worked for FDR, and it would likely work again. During this same period, we also gained some of our greatest national parks and monuments. Electric cars are coming, and gas and diesel will go the way of the steam train, relegated to museums and collectors.

An associate of mine, Rick, predicts that one day all the guys who have vintage gasoline-powered vehicles will tow them down to an enclosed coliseum to show them, to contain the pollution. We laugh, but he may be right.

Battery technology has gotten off to a slow start. The Arabs may have had the first batteries, at least on this planet, around AD 300. Not much happened between then and 1800. The lead acid was born around that time. Thomas Edison came up with a better nickel iron battery, which the Germans improved on; it became the nickel cadmium. There were not many improvements from 1900 to 1970. Then came mercury, sulfur sodium, and finally lithium chloride, along with various types of fuel cells. It still took another thirty years for the lithium's to get to market. But now there are teams of scientists all over the world using a wide variety of technologies and competing to make the best battery. Capacitors have been improved by several orders of magnitude and are even catching up to some batteries. The merger of nanotechnology, carbon fiber technology, and ultra capacitor technology are making progress.

CHAPTER 15

Nuke It!

I believe it is inevitable that someone will figure how to use resonant frequency to rattle matter apart and capture the energy in a nonnuclear process. A gram of dirt has enough energy to run your car for a year. Atoms may be really small, but even the simplest elements like hydrogen and helium, which only have a couple of electrons on each atom, have enough power to push a truck across a state.

There are—correction, *were*—two distinct groups of physicists. One group was trying to take atoms apart, and the other was trying to put atoms back together. That's an oversimplification. The basic building blocks of most of the elements we are familiar with are protons, neutrons, and electrons. All the roughly 120 elements that man is familiar with are made of some combination of these three building blocks. You can take the electrons, protons, and neutrons from an oxygen molecule and reassemble them into a helium molecule, with some leftover parts. If you imagine a long line with the guys who are trying to master dissembling atoms at one end, and the guys who are trying to master reassembling atoms on the other end, they are working their way toward each other and will eventually run into each other. Large particle accelerators are the tools of these parties. In the fifties, one of these teams added the proper number of components to an atom of lead and turned it into gold. Shortly before that, the other group built the first nuclear reactors. Take it apart; put it back together. Taking apart the huge, complex, and perhaps more unstable elements like uranium, strontium, radium, and plutonium comes with a lot of loose ends and is messy. The spare particles generated tend to stick to things and are hazardous to most life forms. But there are still almost one hundred other elements with almost as much energy locked up in them. I believe it is a matter of time, and lots of diligent research will allow us to strip off the power from some of these other elements without the nasty side effects.

When we master the atom, we get a sort of free bonus. Matter can be converted to energy, and energy can be converted to matter. There is no written or unwritten law that says all these process will inherently produce destructive radiation. Take tin, for example. It has about half the protons, neutrons, and electrons that uranium has. Early on, one might jump to the conclusion that some law, like the law of conservation of energy, might require that it takes as much energy to break those bonds as is contained in the bonds. That notion was disproved by a bunch of mathematicians and physicists in New Mexico at a place called Alamogordo shortly before World War II ended. The current nuclear technology has serious hazards associated with it, but it will likely be the stepping stone to some nuclear processes that do not have the same undesirable by-products.

Fire is a nuclear process of sorts. Two elements combine in such a way as to release heat and light. But it does not generate enough of the bad types of ionizing radiation, that nasty stuff that sticks to things, to be considered harmful. Most scientists like to discern between chemical reactions and nuclear reactions, but the net effects are strikingly similar. There's a pretty fair chance that one can find nonradioactive methods of stripping the high-energy electrons off atoms.

CHAPTER 16

The Great ALCAN Junkyard

In 1942, the United States built the ALCAN Highway. ALCAN is an acronym for Alaska-Canadian highway. It's about 1,300 miles long today, but when they first built it, it was 1,700 miles long. It starts way up in Northern British Columbia at Dawson Creek, runs through the Yukon Territory, and heads into Alaska, ending in Delta Junction. Most of the highway is in Canada, with less than two hundred miles in Alaska. Most of Alaska and much of Northern British Columbia, as well as the Yukon, are beyond the area where it is practical to recycle. If iron and steel are worth five bucks a ton, and it is going to cost you twenty-five bucks a ton to haul it to a recycling facility or a shipping port, it's not going to happen. Therefore Alaska and much of Canada are littered with cars, trucks, washing machines, refrigerators, stoves—you name it. Some houses along the ALCAN had to make their own power. A generator might only last two or three years, so outside the houses are huge rows of dead generators, a couple of washers and dryers, refrigerator, and a bunch of dead cars. The United States is sometimes referred to as the Saudi Arabia of scrap. That's because America uses more stuff and generates more scrap than any other country. To countries like China, Japan, and Korea, who want the used metal, paper, and plastic, the United States is a gold mine. Those guys would love the ALCAN! They recycle the scrap back into raw material to make more stuff, which they often sell back to us. It's usually a great deal cheaper than mining ore and processing it into new metal. When a container of shoes comes over from Asia, that container will go back to Asia full of scrap. Not too many people live in Alaska, and along the ALCAN in Canada, there are not many containers full of stuff going up, with practically no empty containers full of scrap coming back down. The scrap simply stays there. If you travel around Alaska or drive the ALCAN, it looks like the entire world is a junk yard. In central Alaska and throughout interior Canada, even the rarer, more expensive metals like aluminum and copper don't always get recycled. You might have to wait five years for the price to go up enough to barely make a profit. Everywhere man goes, he leaves behind a bunch of junk.

When they first started to build the Alaska Pipeline and develop the Prudhoe Bay Oil Field, the government passed legislation making the pipeline and oil companies put up "contingency fund" money to guarantee that things get cleaned up. If the contractors building the pipeline built a camp for the workers that cost $50 million, then they had to put up $50 million more into a savings account. Once they no longer needed the camp, they were required to remove it, remediate the spot, replant it, and pretty much restore it to how it was before they got there. Then, and only then, they got their fifty million back, plus interest. It was usually four or six times what it would cost to remediate the site. If they defaulted, then the state kept the money and cleaned it up themselves. It was a good idea and worked well for many years. But dishonest and sleazy politicians have been making efforts to steal the money. Much like the mafia stole union pension funds, the state is trying to make off with the money. When they established the Permanent Dividend

Fund, it was modeled after the Nobel Peace Prize. Nobel invented TNT and made a significant fortune off both manufacturing and leasing out his TNT patents. Upon nearing retirement, he sold a significant portion of his chemical companies. DuPont, his biggest competitor, bought much of Nobel's company. Then Nobel put a large sum of money into a protected savings account of sorts. The Nobel Peace Prize is taken from the interest generated by the massive sum of money, so the principal will always be there. Over the years, the amount has grown. Initially they gave one prize of some amount that was considered significant at the time. Now they award several prizes that are much bigger than the original prize.

Sleazy politicians tried to buy out the Alaskan public with a one-time cash out. Had the Alaskan public fallen for it, they would have lost their permanent dividend forever. Currently, the residents will receive it forever, as will their offspring.

CHAPTER 17

Russian Solar Power

There is a district of Russia that has fairly good soil, but the water is too salty to use. You can't grow crops, you can't use it to cook, and you can't drink it. For some years, water was trucked in via a huge fleet of Mack trucks. Yes, that's right—American-made trucks. Then some brilliant Russian engineer devised a self-distilling water pump that was solar powered. It basically looks like an old-style, lattice construction, windmill tower. It had a big mirror that directed sunlight down into the well. There were a series of angled glass plates. The briny water would evaporate and collect on the bottom of one of the glass plates. Through this evaporation process, the water would stair-step its way up and out of the well. In the process, it was also distilled. Pretty sharp! No moving parts either. They added dye to the well to darken the water and increase the evaporation rate. Over time, the dye would collect in the surface tank. Servicing consisted of cleaning the glass plates once or twice a year, as well as shoveling the dye back down into the well. They were able to sell off the entire fleet of water-tanker trucks, and the area became more habitable as well as able to grow more crops. It also eliminated some fuel use by the fleet of now decommissioned trucks. Sometimes simple, older technology is the answer.

CHAPTER 18

Coming Up with a Solution

There are plenty of whiners and complainers on this planet. Complaining about a problem doesn't get you anywhere. You fix it, repair it, modify it, or invent a new process or new technology to solve the problem. Those who march in protest are generally totally ineffective and are usually becoming more of the problem.

Here are two current examples. The first revolves around some oil exploration that is in the Arctic. Protestors get in kayaks that are entirely a product of the petrochemical industry, with paddles and safety vest that are also plastic, a product straight out of the petrochemical stream. They paddle around trying to blockade these massive offshore oil rigs. They put themselves in harm's way, and for what? Just to get attention? Did they change any policy? No. Did they stop anybody? No. But they did use up fuel to get there, and they did get there in a vehicle that was a product of the petrochemical industry. Yes, they did take pictures with their cell phones that are almost 100 percent out of the petrochemical stream. Yes, their pictures in the paper are printed with ink straight out of the chemical stream. I work in the electrical industry. We use as much or more plastic than we do copper. Computers and electronics in general are totally dependent on plastics for insulation, and plastic is 100 percent out of the petrochemical stream. Protestors say, "The people have a right to be informed. The public needs to know," or any of a million other totally moot, illogical excuses. The people who are in the know are thinking to themselves, "What idiots, what boneheads!" Is that what you are going to put on your resume? If you take pride in doing really stupid stuff, I'm probably not going to hire you.

Chaim Herzog said," It is ignorance that creates problems, With knowledge come solutions." Protestors complaining about problems simply become part of the problem. If you really want to make a difference, you have to do something about it! Go to school, become a researcher, invent a better battery, find plastic alternatives, or solve energy problems. There are an infinite number of solutions, but complaining and protesting are not part of the solution. The whiners, complainers, and protestors are part of the problem. They are *not* part of the solution. There are plenty of people who don't want something. Fine, but you have to come up with an alternative or substitute. You may be willing to live without transportation, medicine, and all the modern conveniences, but most of the people on this planet want that stuff and are going to run over you if you try to block them from having it. Maybe you can live off the grid, but most folks have to drive to work, and they want to use their cell phones, and they are not going to be too interested in giving up most of that stuff. God forbid you try to stop Mom from taking her kid to the doctor! That's not happening!

The second example is the proposal to build some new pipeline somewhere. Okay, think it through. If you don't build the line, what are the alternatives? Oh, you didn't think that far ahead? Here's what happens. They haul the material by rail and truck. By rail takes roughly twice the fuel, so the pollution produced by going by rail will be twice as much in the long run. Now you are burning twice the fuel, producing twice the pollution. How did that work out for you? By truck the cost and fuel usage, as well as pollution produced, goes up to three times as much. If you did your homework, you would find that more of the product, regardless of what it is, will be spilled by truck and by rail. The media does not report every truck or train accident, but pipeline accidents get the front page. Simply because you didn't hear about it, that doesn't mean it didn't happen. The medical industry is also heavily dependent on plastics. Those who want to revert back to the "old ways" seem to forget that without all this "stuff," they are only going to live about two-thirds as long. Lots of folks know what they don't want, like a nuke in their backyard or a pipeline. However, if you can't suggest an alternative, then voicing a dissenting opinion really serves no purpose.

Results yield respect.
—Clark Kellogg

George Washington Carver created oil out of soybeans. He even created some soy-based plastic. He made greater improvements in his lifetime than all the efforts of all the protestors in all of history since the beginning of time. A wise man would take up where he left off.

Carver anticipated the destruction wrought by the boll weevil. In its move eastward into the cotton-producing states, he realized that it would put farms and farm workers out of work. Did he protest? Hell no. He came up with a solution. He traveled extensively throughout the Southern cotton-producing states and convinced many farmers to switch to peanuts and soybeans. Those who took his advice came out far better than those who ignored him. The farmhands whom he was trying to protect still had jobs and could feed their families—also an important consideration.

Carver sets the perfect example:

1) He identified the problem.

2) He came up with realistic solutions.

3) He worked to institute those solutions.

You will notice that he did not waste his time by protesting or complaining. George Washington Carver earned respect. Protestors, whiners, complainers, and strikers do not earn respect or change things.

A major stepping stone to decreasing pollution is increasing efficiency. If you can perform a task with half the energy, then you produce half the pollution. This is a good field to get in if you want to make a difference.

Inventors ultimately solve lots of problems, so become an inventor. To be an effective inventor, it is best to first look at and see what some other guy did first.

CHAPTER 19

Not Invented Here (NIH)

Some technicians and engineers at one of the nation's nuclear facilities needed a special crane for a very specific application. They modified some existing design, and it worked nicely. It also saved them a bunch of money. A process engineer of my acquaintance worked on the project. Later, when he was working at another facility on the opposite coast, they needed that same piece of equipment, but they adamantly refused to copy the one from the previous place. They insisted they develop it themselves. They spent ten times as much of the taxpayers' money—and then it didn't work.

In the seventies shortly after some major power outage and an oil embargo, federal agencies gave all kinds money and grants for solar and wind research. But the majority of the research grants were a waste of time, energy, and money because the folks doing the various projects did not bother to research what had already been done. If you started out where the last guy left off, and you only make a 1 percent improvement, you are still points ahead. If you spend millions of dollars on some wind or solar project, and you don't even achieve the level of what some guy did fifty years earlier, then you just wasted a lot of time, money, and effort. There should probably be some guidelines to monitor these projects so that great, expensive resources are not wasted this way.

The reason NIH, or "Not Invented Here," ever came about is partially the government's fault, and here's why. Pick a federal agency—any agency. Their budget is x millions of dollars. If the agency is efficient and honest, and it does not use up all the funds, then Congress will say, "Oh, here's a place they didn't use all their money. We can cut their budget back and save money." But Congress didn't bother to check to see how well that agency performed, how many of their goals they achieved, or how they managed to trim their internal budget. Consequently, every federal agency gets a printout of their current costs, and what percentage of their money they spent, nine months into the year. Then they go out of their way to make sure they spend every cent so that they can get more the next year. I know this because I worked in the guarded room of a government office, where they printed the material. I was undercover, just doing my job, which was wiring up another printer. I've been undercover in more than one industry.

In the construction industry, and probably some other industries like manufacturing, the team that comes in under budget gets the bonus. The guys who didn't perform as well get laid off. I believe that in my entire association with the petrochemical industry, no job was ever completed on time and under budget. In that respect, the oil company executives were a bit like the politicians in that they didn't concern themselves with being on time and under budget. It simply wasn't their problem.

"Not Invented Here" is a crime of inefficiency. I've heard a wide range of bogus justifications for it. Generally it's a waste of someone else's resources, like your and my tax money. Enough on that.

CHAPTER 20

You Didn't Think
of That?

THE LONG–RANGE LOOK AHEAD
AND FUTURE ECONOMICS

Most people, maybe 70 percent of the population, don't look ahead at what the consequences of their actions will be. I've only read about a dozen of these studies. I've participated in a few of these studies, but there are hundreds more that substantiate that percentage. A chess player needs to think ahead several moves ahead. A really good chess player looks ahead seven or eight moves. But, just like the obnoxious TV ad, "It's my money and I want it now!" most folks don't plan too far ahead. Alaskans would sell off all their oil today, given the opportunity. Alaska's politicians have tried too. For the less-informed folks on this planet, you need to be aware that there is a finite, or limited, supply of oil and many other resources. When push comes to shove and these resources start to play out, they will become very expensive. Wars have been fought over resources, from salt to fish to oil.

The oil companies, as well as various governments, have had people looking at these long-range problems for many years. BP did projections in the thirties, forties, and fifties. The CIA operated think tanks in the sixties; these are mathematicians and engineers. If you get enough good data, you can make fairly accurate predictions about the future. Look at a city, check its previous population and then its current population, and come up with a growth rate. This city of 100,000 in 1920 had 150,000 in 1980. It grew by 50 percent in sixty years. Based on this, the engineer can estimate how much electricity will be needed in 2020. He starts building power lines and power plants in anticipation of that point in time. The same is done for water, sewer, roads, and oil. When I was about ten years old, a mathematician (my dad) told me exactly when the population of the earth would be double what it was then. He worked in one of those CIA-run think tanks with a bunch of other smart guys, including some Nobel Laureates. The projection for the doubling time for the population was dead nuts on, or 100 percent correct, almost down to the day.

In the major power struggle between nations, food, water, and oil have serious implications. If we ran out of oil today, you wouldn't be able to drive to work, and the bus couldn't take the kids to school. This would definitely be a problem. The United States has been the biggest hogs when it comes to use of resources, especially oil. We have been the number one consumer of oil since the advent of the oil age, which started around 1900. In 2015, China finally superseded the United States in oil demand. Not too far down the road, India will surpass us too. So what's going to happen when the worldwide demand exceeds the available supply? Are you going to be willing to stay home while someone in India or China drives to work? Not likely. Now, suppose you used up all your own country's oil. You will have to buy it from somewhere else, or generate more expensive synthetic oil. But you are competing with others who want it and are going to have to pay a sky-high price. Isn't there some biblical story about some fair maidens who some used up their oil, and others hoarded and saved their oil? Yeah, maybe someone was thinking about this thousands of years ago.

Now we are going to look at two scenarios. In the first scenario, Alaska sells all its oil. They get rich right now, but their oil is all used up, so they won't make any money in the future. Their kids won't have jobs. And because they were rich, they spent extravagantly. Only a very small percentage save their money and spend it wisely. It's not half, or even one-quarter—it tends to be a small percentage. The net effect is that a bunch of Alaskans are out of work and broke. That's not good, as these things go.

Now we'll look at the second scenario, which is the winning chess move. They buy the other guy's oil and sit on their oil. This isn't good for the economy right now, because money is leaving the country and not coming back. But further down the road, the other guy's oil runs out. Now you still have some oil, and the price is so high that you get what you previously spent back—with interest! What's more, you don't have to fight a war or compete with some other nation for it. You already have it. But the majority doesn't care, doesn't understand, and doesn't realize that they would be cutting their kids out of a future, basically losing the war by following their greedy instincts. In this way, the majority of people end up like lemmings jumping into the sea, or buffalo being run off a cliff by well-organized Indians. Alaskans may be insulted or offended by this, but they did it before; they definitely already went down that road. Humans have a very specific history of making the same mistakes over and over again.

In a well-documented report in a fire journal, more than half of the people confronted by a bacon fire on their stove threw water on it and that sloshed out the grease all over the stove—making an even bigger fire. Only a small percentage of the people lifted up the pan and set it in the sink, which is the correct move. This happens so frequently that in one place, I installed a massive electric gate entering a neighborhood so that the fire department could take a shortcut from the firehouse to put out these fires. They reported one or two a week.

This first reaction type, often referred to as a knee-jerk reaction, is very often a mistake. Those who plan ahead need to make sure that the next generation is aware of the importance of these actions. In northern California, the fathers of the owners of a saw mill purchased huge swaths of forest rich with cedar and redwood. They made the investment in anticipation of things being slow at the saw mill. When things got slow, they could cut their own timber. But the sons and daughters sold the mill, along with all the timber property. It sold for a pittance—just the price of the mill. Some banker in New York, not a lumber man, noticed that the sale included all this timber property, and he snapped it up for next to nothing. He paid something like $50,000 and got several million in redwood and cedar, not to mention thousands of acres of land. The greedy kids just gave it away. Not too smart. The banker in New York was listed as the entrepreneur of the year in Fortune or Forbes. For this reason, it is important for these strategic plans to be passed on to the future generations, lest they are forgotten.

There are many documented cases of politicians waiting to see what the public wants before making a decision. They may be more concerned with getting reelected than making the right decision. Consequently, if one goes with the public's cries and demands, the wrong decision is made, and we are headed down the wrong path. By not looking ahead in this way, many people are destroying any possibility of a future for their offspring. They may not know it or be aware of the consequences, but they are still guilty. Now, the politician is not going to spell it out to you in such blunt terms even if he knows, because it's not what you want to hear, and it won't get him votes.

CHAPTER 21

Facts versus Opinion

Opinions are like hot air: they are here, and then they are gone. More than half the time, they are wrong. People form opinions based on no data, limited data, and incorrect data all the time, and so their opinions are very often incorrect. People usually believe what they want to believe, and will often find a way to discredit the truth if it is not what they want to hear.

If you participated in debating in High School, one of the things they teach you is to reference your sources. In the late 60's and early 70's Playboy and Esquire were considered a "Creditable" source. Today the News Media has become more of a propaganda and opinion brainwashing machine. Quite a significant amount of information on the Internet is also incorrect. For instance one source claimed that Christian Heretics perpetrated some event in 69 BC. O.K. What's wrong with that statement? How can you have Christians before Christ? Yeah, right. In recent times the media has definitely become more proficient at Brainwashing and brow-beating the public into believing all sorts of stuff that isn't even remotely close to the truth. Citing sources becomes a moot point when the reader has been so infused with false information that they refuse to believe what is real. If it is not what they want to hear they will be the first ones to try to discredit the source by claiming that it is run by some opposition party. If people are that hard headed, and are refusing to believe the truth, why bother citing sources? They have made it clear that they are not going to believe it anyway.

Psychology studies indicate that if you tell someone something over and over, even if its not true people will believe it and act on it. Other people in these same fields couldn't believe it so they did their own studies and got the same results. Advertisers, Politicians, and people with questionable ulterior motives use these techniques,… on you and everyone else. A huge portion of the population has been led to believe all sorts of stuff that isn't true.

What we tell up and coming apprentice electricians is: "If you don't know,… Look it up", this is usually in reference to the Code, and rules that electrical installations are made under. Something I've been teaching for over 30 years.

Facts are concrete. They are like the pyramids and withstand the test of time. Someone's opinion from a hundred years ago isn't even recorded in a document, but the pyramids are still there. Much of the material in the media is not based on facts. Much of it has flaws in reasoning and flaws in logic, meant to trick even the sharpest of individuals. I refer to two lists of flaws in reasoning and flaws of logic when watching a newscast, and I have seen what claims to be news contains less than 20 percent actual facts. One list is fallacies that may sound logical but are not. There are forty with their respective Latin names. The other is intellectually honest and intellectually dishonest debate tactics, with some fifty-five examples. You can find them on the Internet, and they are used in business and law classes. My motto is "Test everything." The sixties version was "Question authority." In my racket, I test with precision meters and instruments—ones that are accurate. Those meters and instruments have calibration certificates that verify and attest to the accuracy of the instrument. They get recalibrated on a regular basis. Pictures are a good method of documenting things.

An associate of mine, a full PhD professor who teaches at a university, calls news channels Faux Newz. I have to laugh, but he's right.

"Don't believe everything you see, or hear." That's a quote from four thousand years ago, from the Old Testament. It was good advice back then and is still applicable today.

I deal mostly in facts, statistics, and stuff that has been checked and checked again. It is in my nature as an inspector. I also grew up with mathematicians and other scientists who are seeking the truth. As an inspector, I witness, verify, document, test, and take pictures. I deal in what really happened, not some opinion. If you read something you don't agree with, or something you didn't want to hear or don't want to believe, then you'd better do some research and check it out before you claim that something is false. You may not like what you find, but it is often more important to know the truth. Your life could depend on it.

If I'm going to swing on a rope swing over some canyon, I want to know unequivocally that the rope is going to hold, that the tree is strong enough. Maybe I'd request to see a "load test" certificate. Your opinion? I'm not even interested unless you are the rope manufacturer, or the engineer who designed the swing, and then I might listen. But odds are I'm still going to inspect it myself.

CHAPTER 22

The Inspector!

Arguing with an inspector is like wrestling with
a pig in the mud. After a while you come to
realize that the pig likes it!

—author unknown

Get up around four in the morning, seven days a week. Work out on two elliptical and two pedal machines, have breakfast, shave, and suit up with fire-retardant clothing. In the winter, which is three-quarters of the year in Prudhoe, start your truck. When it's forty below, the seat is like a concrete park bench, only colder and harder. It'll take an hour for the truck to warm up. Attend one or even two safety meetings, one for the client and another for your company. You might have some morning meetings to review ongoing work, do planning and scheduling for some future work, and review the plans for upcoming jobs.

This review process is quite important. An engineering firm will generate some plans for the new addition or whatever the project is, and then all the different trades—pipefitters, mechanics, electricians, welders, carpenters, scaffold builders, engineers, and safety people—sit down and review them. They often catch multimillion-dollar mistakes. They assess for safety. What would happen if ...? How many permits, and what type? Does the system satisfy any of a million different codes and standards? Is it OSHA compliant? Code of federal regulations, NEC, ASME, and NFPA?

After the review, the plans will be sent back to the engineering firm for revisions. Often they will go through this review one or two more times before being approved for construction. When they get the final "issue for construction" stamp, they will likely have a dozen signatures by approval authorities and engineers of various disciplines. That is all before any of a dozen different permits are issued to start construction. Quality assurance and quality control inspectors (QA and QC), as well as safety inspectors, start watching the work. If you are an inspector, you keep a log book or diary. I still have the last ten years of spiral-bound notebooks. Based on my notes, I also generate a daily report that goes to all the foreman, project managers, bosses, schedulers, and planners. It's done electronically and filed. I retain a copy of it as well. This makes it difficult for anyone to hide or cover up something. QC and QA both document it. The foreman has it in his own daily report, as does the project manager and the safety guy. If you compare these five reports and there are any discrepancies, someone is probably going to get fired—not always, but most of the time.

In a common example, a welder gets something in his eye. The craft-hands (other workers) try to cover it up. The welder is eventually forced to go to the medic because his eye is serious. Both the client and the contractors are likely to fire the project managers, foreman, safety guy, and employee. I've witnessed it over a dozen times.

A lot of times, no one actually reads my daily reports. Periodically I would inject something funny into the report. On one occasion, the vice president of the United States was touring the VMT. That's the southern terminal of the Alaska Pipeline or Valdez Marine Terminal. They were being shown around by one of the security people in a big van. When they went by where I was inspecting, they waved. On my daily report, I put "Met with vice president and the governor, discussed state of the nation," When my boss got back from R & R, he sent me an e-mail asking if he could get invited next time!

CHAPTER 23

The Little Guy versus the Big Guy

Big Oil is usually referring to the supermajors. These are the top players, and usually counted in their ranks are Chevron, Exxon/Mobile, Dutch Royal Shell, Total SA, BP, Eni, and more recently Conoco-Phillips. They have net worth and gross sales that are more than the GNP of many countries. They are somewhat interlinked. Each of these huge companies owns huge blocks of stock in the car manufacturing companies, as well as in each other. As a consequence of this, most of them are not going to do anything that upsets the apple cart, so to speak. They regulate prices, and they use that ability to force the smaller players out of business so that they can buy them out. This has been going on since the beginning of the oil industry.

As previously mentioned, these big players can afford to employ all manner of safety and environmental people, and they do. The smaller, far more competitive companies don't always have the deep pockets the big guys do, and they have to cut costs wherever they can. The smaller companies tend to cover up more spills more than the big players.

In one case I was privy to, one of the big companies spilled maybe a hundred gallons of fuel, and it made the front page of the papers as well as the national TV news networks. On the same day, a small contractor that was a subcontractor to the oil companies spilled thirty thousand gallons of fuel. There was no investigation, and it was not mentioned in the news. The subcontractor did report it to the correct federal agency, but it incorrectly reported that it was under fifty gallons. The representative from the federal agency didn't come right away to look at the spill, and the contractor parked heavy equipment all over the spot. That same evening, there was a massive arctic storm that covered the spill with a foot of snow. By spring, the oil had seeped into the ground, and no one was the wiser.

This was not an isolated case. When the little companies screw up, there is far more of a tendency to cover it up. The big guys pay the fines; the little guys can't afford to pay the fines, and so they hide it. I've known the big companies to pay fines in advance, as well as fines for spills that never occurred. Alyeska paid a fine for spilling ten thousand gallons of propane, but it turned out to be a faulty gauge. They didn't spill a drop.

Halon, as a fire-extinguishing agent, was banned after a certain date. It's a chlorofluorocarbon similar to Freon, but it's the best firefighting agent. BP, Alyeska, and ARCO bought up the entire world's supply and paid the fifty dollars per pound fine for using it, in advance.

Most of what Americans hear about are domestic spills in the United States and neighboring waters. On the Internet, you can find detailed lists of most of the spills since the 1950s. The *Exxon Valdez* wasn't even in the top twenty. For many years, the largest spill in recorded history was a spill in the Gulf of Mexico, near the US–Mexico border. It was the I-TOX One spill of 1977. Once you get out of the United States, all bets are off. In many foreign countries, spills never make the news. There are places in the world where they have had a dozen spills the size of the recent incident in the Gulf.

In the case of the *Deepwater Horizon,* the "smaller company" was Halliburton, which is not really a small company. They were hired by BP to drill the well, and they screwed up. BP took the hit because it was their lease, but they didn't really cause the spill—their subcontractor did. Halliburton is a very politically connected company, especially to many previous US presidents, senators, and congressmen. No politician is going to step up to the plate and admit that a US company that has a long history of clandestine operations, and that pours money into politicians pockets, screwed up. It's interesting how a big oil company becomes the fall guy for covering up clandestine operations by the government, but that's another story.

Another interesting observation is the following. If the State of Alaska had become an oil company, they would have become the seventh- or eighth-largest oil company in the world. That would have netted them yearly profits in the billions of dollars—significantly more than what it costs to run the state. Instead, they squandered away a small percentage of that. Eventually they overtaxed the oil companies, forcing them out of the state. Not very bright. It certainly does not reflect very well on their politicians.

CHAPTER 24

The Goldfinger Scenario

In the James Bond thriller *Goldfinger*, the villain, Auric Goldfinger, is a gold bullion dealer. His plan is to nuke Fort Knox, making that gold radioactive for ninety-nine years and thereby increasing the market value of his gold. This almost happened in 1991, except it was oil. "Madman Insane," or Saddam Hussein, started firing missiles at Israel. Israel has had nuclear capabilities for quite some time, and they were getting pissed off. Their hand was on the button, so to speak. If they nuked Kuwait and Saddam, the oil in that region would be radioactive and unusable for a long time. The price of oil worldwide would likely have doubled, leading to economic crisis. What if you suddenly had to pay six bucks a gallon for gas? What if you couldn't get gas? Almost every NATO nation, and several outside of NATO, stepped in and squashed the attack. They had no intention of letting that happen. Even unlikely players like Russia stepped in. It's astounding how many players stepped up to the plate on that one. It could also have had something to do with the Gulf War lasting only from August 1990 to February 1991.

The next military engagement in the Middle East was enough of a threat that where I was working, North America's largest oil field, they brought in crews and pulled long-dormant, older drill rigs out of storage, preparing to get drilling in case we got cut off from our oil coming from the Middle East. We normally had a dozen to two dozen operating drill rigs in Prudhoe, but right up until one of the military actions, we had close to all seventy-three rigs up and ready to go. It was impressive. Nobody told us why. As soon as the crisis in the Middle East was over, those rigs were "stacked," the term for being shut down and stored away for future use. The crews were sent home. But somebody was anticipating trouble. Simply because you never heard about it, that does not mean it didn't happen. I could introduce you to five hundred witnesses, the guys brought in to man the long-dormant drill rigs. There were closer to two thousand workers already working on the slope at the time. There had to be another one thousand engineers and economists in the government, and working for the big oil companies around the globe, who knew all about this too. It was a lot more serious than most people knew.

CHAPTER 25

Shutting Down
Alaska

This isn't another one of those O'Reilly "Killing" books, but it *is* serious. There are a lot of environmentalists out there who are about to cheer. Well, don't rejoice just yet. We are back to our complex chess game, where the wrong move now can cost you the whole game. This game is about power and money, and it's being played on a global scale.

When I first started working in Alaska, I flew from Seattle to Anchorage every two, three, or four weeks, according to the rotation schedule I was on and according to the wishes of my alternate. While I was at home, on R & R, there was another person who held the same certifications, licenses, and credentials as I did, and he was doing my job. He had my truck, my office, my computer, and my room at the camp. He was me, when I wasn't there. If his daughter was getting married, or if his kid was graduating, we might juggle our schedules so that he could be off at that time. We often took turns for who was off at Christmas, New Years, Fourth of July, and other holidays. This meant I flew the 2,600 miles each way a minimum of eight or nine round trips a year. Usually it was more like twelve, and if I worked a two-and-two rotation, that moved up to twenty-six. On every flight, we flew right up the coast of Alaska. From the jet at thirty thousand feet, one can get a pretty good view of some of Alaska's larger glaciers. There are over a thousand. Some are the size of Rhode Island. Some are seventy-five miles long. What I noticed most was the alarming rate at which they were receding. From the Alaska Air jet, they still looked big from our vantage point. Nestled back in giant canyons, they were melting away right before our eyes, often right out of sight. In at least one case, tour boats could no longer get to where the ice was "calving." It seemed to speed up over the years. It would be pretty hard to convince me that global warming doesn't have anything to do with it.

Meanwhile, back up in Prudhoe Bay, it was evident another way. The entire North Slope butts right into the Beaufort Sea. It's very flat. You can see to the horizon in any direction. In the winter, with the ocean frozen, it is hard to tell where the land ends and the ocean starts. In the summer, which is brief but has twenty-four-hour days, the sea ice melts back. When I first started working there in 1994, the open area between the permanently frozen sea ice and the land was often only five miles wide, so I could see the ice of the North Pole. The real North Pole is a further 1,600 miles north. As time elapsed, the sea ice receded farther and farther. Some summers the band of open water was twenty miles wide. One could still see the permanent sea ice, but it was over the horizon, and what one was really seeing was a mirage, a sort of thermal inversion that allowed one to see over the horizon. It always made the ice look twice as tall as it actually was. The environment is changing at an accelerated rate. It's been quite noticeable over the twenty-one years I worked there.

I am familiar with about twenty-six oil facilities in and around Prudhoe Bay that each cost between $10 and $100 billion. Besides that, there are at least one thousand miles of aboveground pipelines that carry oil, gas, and water. Everything built on the North Slope oil patch is up on stilts. The entire 1,500 square miles of the developed oil field sits on permafrost that is 1,000–3,000 feet thick. By definition, permafrost is any land that is continuously frozen for over a year. Drilling and core sampling indicates that it's more like millions of years, not just since the last ice age cycle. I believe ice age cycles are roughly eleven thousand years. Every pipeline and perhaps a thousand buildings, camps, processing modules, fire control modules, compressors, turbines, and pumps are all on vertical support members. A VSM is basically a piece of pipe ranging from four to forty inches in diameter that has had one end welded shut with a piece of flat plate. To support pipelines and modules, one drills a hole in the ground larger than the VSM you are going to install. You drop in the VSM, and then a specialized variation of a concrete truck backs up to the hole and pours in slurry. The concrete truck has been insulated with spray-on urethane foam, and the slurry is a mixture of hot water, sand, and gravel. This mixture closely resembles what you drilled out of the permafrost in the first place. Now you drop a thermocouple, an electric temperature sensor, in and wait for it to freeze. It is done when it's usually between twenty to forty below zero, and it takes a couple of days to set up. Then you backfill around the top with tundra soil and reseed it with tundra seed provided by the state and federal governments.

I worked all over the slope: Bedalmi, Endicott, North Star, the EOA, the WOA, Point Mac, STP, CPS, CGF, Kuparuk, North Star, MPU, Alpine, and Eni. There are only a few places that I didn't work. The last ten years, I flew in to one of the two airports, Dead Horse and Kuparuk, and drove the remaining thirty-eight or fifteen miles, respectively, to my camp and office. Regardless of which way I came in, I drove along the Kuparuk Pipeline. Kuparuk is the third largest oil field on the North Slope. It was developed later than the larger EOA and WOA fields. All the oil from the respective fields goes to pump 1, the start of the Alaska Pipeline. There are at least seven pipelines that all terminate at pump 1. One in particular, the Kuparuk line, is a fairly good-sized line, and it was installed on VSMs that are sinking into the permafrost. I drove by it on a daily to weekly basis. Every winter, crews went out and jacked up the pipeline with air bags and jacks, and then they put cribbing under it. This takes the weight off the VSM, which can then be raised back up or extended. In the summer, the Kuparuk pipeline looks like a roller coaster, and when the crews get done in the winter, it's back to flat, straight, and level as a pool table. The VSMs are not painted in most cases, so they are rust brown. In the summer they absorb heat. Steel conducts heat, so now they melt their way back into the permafrost. I'm a bit surprised they didn't paint them white or silver so that they didn't suck up as much heat. That may be coming. I guess they will need a bunch of painters! With literally thousands of miles of pipelines and modules weighing in at two thousand tons sitting on hundreds of these VSMs, it's going to be a big problem when they all start settling into the ground.

The events that lead to a disaster are usually not single events, but a domino chain of events. When they first started operating the Trans-Alaska Pipeline, enough hot oil was going through it that freezing was not a problem. It's insulated the whole length. The oil comes out of the ground hot, between one hundred and two hundred degrees. Some heat is lost in processing. The oil contains water, sand, and a bunch of crap you don't want, so you refine that out before shipping it. Also, you try to get rid of anything that will be detrimental to the piping system, like corrosive H_2S or abrasive sand. The massive 17,500-horsepower pumps at each of the ten operating pump stations added back in about a degree of heat. But in the worst-case scenario—say, in the dead of winter, with forty below ambient temperatures—if the line was to shut down because of some unplanned emergency like a break, damage from seismic activity, or fire at one of the pump stations, it could be curtains for Alaska. Originally the studies showed that they would have close to forty days to repair the line. After that, the oil would gel up and freeze, plugging the line. Restarting the line was estimated to take an entire year. One would have to drill into the low spots and somehow suck out or soften up with hot fluids the frozen and gelled spots. Shutting down the pipeline for a year would have disastrous effects on Alaska, as well as a worldwide economic impact.

It gets much worse. Alaska politicians passed the ACES tax legislation, which raised oil taxes to higher than any other US state or any other foreign country in the world. It was based primarily on the barrel throughput of the Trans-Alaska Pipeline. But it was also dependent on the barrel price at market. If the price of oil ever reached $130 a barrel, all the operators on the North Slope would be operating at a loss. One can't stay in business that way. The investors and stock shareholders of the respective oil companies all said, "Get our money out of Alaska! Put it in some other oil field, like the North Sea, Saudi Arabia, or the Gulf of Mexico, where we can make money!" The initial effect was that it bankrupted several dozen little suppliers and subcontractors in Alaska, mostly in Anchorage.

But an oil field needs constant attention and maintenance to the tune of millions of dollars. The oil companies tapered back to pumping just enough oil to barely keep the fields alive. This in turn moved that critical worst-case scenario from forty days down to ten, and then below even that. The pipeline started installing heating equipment all along the line because they were worried. There is yet another complication. Whenever you shut down an oil well, it usually does not produce as well when you start it back up. At one facility that I worked at, we had about four hundred working wells: some gas, some producers, and some injectors. If there was a power outage or some sort of equipment failure that resulted in an emergency shutdown, we almost always lost a well, one of our producers. They would plug up with sand, or the pump would quit and not restart. It cost $2 million to bring in the well rig, pull out the two to seven miles of pipe, fix the well, and put it back together. If it was a fifty barrel per day well, it would take one thousand days of production to pay for that. If the Trans-Alaska Pipeline shuts down for more than a couple of days, the entire ten thousand wells on the North Slope would have to be shut down because there is no place to put the oil. As temperatures rise—which they visibly are on the North Slope—the entire infrastructure, sitting on half a million VSMs, all start sinking into the ground. That could lead to serious spills, and it could shut down the largest oil field in North America.

There are indications that this is happening. Several of the big players have been trying to sell out and get out of dodge. One of the oil companies brought in a contingent of Russians, who looked distinctly like Russian mob, to look it over. Ownership of some facilities has changed. Shareholders are probably not going to be interested in paying for some massive, expensive cleanup and repairs to make it right. Gigs like the *Deepwater Horizon* and the *Exxon Valdez* are not your first option if you are an oil company.

Environmental groups might jump to the conclusion that they have just won a great victory, but think about the consequences. People and industries will still want and need oil. They will simply get it from some other field. But no matter how you factor it, getting it from another source will create more pollution. Whether it comes by ship, rail, or truck, it will almost certainly use more fuel to transport than it would by coming down the Alaska pipeline, especially for California, Oregon, Washington, Hawaii, and parts of Idaho and Montana. Washington, Oregon, Alaska, and Hawaii used to get 100 percent of their oil from Alaska. If it shuts down, where is the oil going to come from? Probably farther away. Transporting it farther is going to burn more fuel, which is going to produce more carbon dioxide, so that didn't work out so well.

Things are melting down so fast in the polar regions that they are anticipating and building for a new northern trade route across the top of the globe. Canada, the United States, Greenland, Iceland, Norway, Sweden, Finland, and Russia have put together a consortium to control it. They are building ice cutters. They are rebuilding old Arctic outposts and military installations, and they're building new installations, in anticipation of the new Northwest Passage—the very one that Humble Oil's SS *Manhattan* opened up. The ice is melting, and they are betting on it in a big way. If the oil companies start taking oil out of the massive Navy Petroleum Reserve #4, or PET 4 for short, they may bypass the Trans-Alaska pipeline altogether. This means Alaska would not get anything. No oil tariff for Alaska. They are actively trying to block any construction around that area, including issuing a permit to build a huge tank farm where they could store months of production, west of Barrow, Alaska, to later be hauled out by ship. Alaska is in a precarious position. Their prize oil field could turn into a huge mud pie. In half a dozen scenarios, production could zero out, along with all of Alaska's income, and the main players are all bailing out. It's time to get out the silver paint! Tom Sawyer would have a field day with this one. We are not talking about painting a little fence—it's like a fence two thousand miles long.

There's more oil and gas in the Yukon Territory and the Northwest Territory. The pipeline they were going to build for that was cancelled. That oil could go out the same way, by tanker, through the fabled Northwest Passage. If the governments of seven countries and a dozen oil companies are making plans and spending millions of dollars in preparation for something dependent on global warming, I'd be inclined to believe that it is happening.

Acronyms

The oil companies, much like the military, use a lot of three- and four-letter acronyms to designate places and programs. There is little standardization, and sometime the same letter combinations are reused for something entirely different. PPE (personnel protective equipment) is one example. The Trans-Alaska Pipeline had a bunch of these specific to the pipeline.

PLQ: Permanent living quarters. Nice camps at the eleven pump stations, on the level of three- or four-star hotels.

ARTS Radio: Alyeska radio telephone system. Precursor to cell phones; private radio system.

SA–38: Their safety program. It required a four-inch binder. Their quality program, formerly QA 36 and later QA 136, was also a huge, comprehensive document. With the pipeline, it was all about procedure. BP, ARCO, Conoco Phillips, Exxon Mobile, and Shell had their own equivalent documents.

JPO: Joint Pipeline Office. Seventeen federal and state agencies that oversee the Trans-Alaska Pipeline.

Psalm SA 38

Big Oil is my shepherd; I shall not whine.

He maketh me to line down in the PLQ. He leadeth me to the sauna.

He restoreth my bank account and leadeth me in the path of economic security.

Yea, though I drive through the frozen treeless tundra, I will fear no breakdown, for thou ARTS radio is with me. Thy CB and thy arctic gear will comfort me.

Thou preparest a steak as I watch mine enemies on CNN. Thou fuelest my Mercedes.

Surely JPO and the tree huggers have followed me all the days of my career and I will take a package and retire from the House of Big Oil forever.

Some Source Material

Cronkite, Walter. *A Reporter's Life.* New York: Ballantine Books, 1997.

Personal History, Katharine Graham

Electrified Oil Production, Howell & Hogwood

Modern Oil Well Pumping, Zaba

An American Hero, Singerman

Beyond Oil, Deffeyes

The Great Alaska Pipeline, Stan Cohen

Crossing Alaska, Michael Gilders

Pipeline Stories, Dermot Cole

The Great Wildcatter, Sam T Mallison

My American Journey, Colin Powell

The Grid, SC Hewe

2011 NEC, NFPA 70.

Electrical World & Engineer 43, no. 3 (January 1904).

The Story of the Bell System, PT & T, 1930

Dynamo Electric Machinery, Samuel Sheldon, 1905

Mathematics for Electricity & Radiomen, Cooke

Master Book of Tables and Formulas, Martin Clifford

Aids to Engineers Examinations, Hawkins, 1897

Electric Machinery and Transformers, Irving Hosow

International Library of Technology, Steam Engine Pumps, 1902

1993 NEC, NFPA 70.

Electrical Motor Controls and Workbook, Gary Rochis, Glen Mazur

Basic Electricity, (US Navy)

2008 NEC, NFPA 70

"Ugly's Electrical Reference"

1901 NEC (reprint)

1897 NEC (reprint)

Pocket Reference, Thomas J Glover

Everyday Glossary of Wire & Cable Terminology, 1967

The National Handbook for Wireman, 1926

Electricity Simplified, Sloan, 1903 (1891)

Handbook of Power Resistors, H.F. Littlejohn 1956

Everyman's Guide to Radio, Yates, 1926

1999 NEC, NFPA 70

WAC Rules, NFPA 79, Grounding & Harmonics, Fault Calculations.

Harmonics and Power Quality

Soars Book on Grounding & Bonding

Traffic Signals & Illumination

Motors, Motor Generators, Synchros, Resolvers, Electronic Servos, Singer

Square D Wiring Diagrams

Antenna Systems

The Lineman's & Cableman's Handbook, Kurtz & Shoemaker

27th, 48th, & 52nd editions of the Handbook of Chemistry and Physics, CRC

2nd Year College Chemistry, Chapin & Steiner

Mathematical Tables from the Handbook of Chemistry and Physics, 1941, CRC.

Hilios, Heine Safety Boiler Co., 1897

Basic Electricity, USD Navy-1960-1970

Radar Electronics Fundamentals, Bureau of Ships, Navy, 1944

How to Test Everything Electronic, Jack Dave

The Electric Circuit, V Karapetoff, 1912

Armature Winding & Motor Repair, Braymer, 1920

Stallcup's Electric Calculations Simplified

Applied Electricity, 1934

Library of Practical Electricity, Vol 1,2,3,4,5,7,&8

1951 NEC Handbook

Alternating Current and Alternating Current Machinery, 1898, T.P. Jackson

A Golden Thread, 2500 years of solar architecture and technology. Ken Butti and John Perlin

And of course: The M.I.T. Library, Jones Library, Robert Frost Library.

www.ingramcontent.com/pod-product-compliance
Lightning Source LLC
Chambersburg PA
CBHW020540290526
45786CB00002B/970